WILD BILL HICKOK
GUNFIGHTER

An Account of Hickok's Gunfights

By

JOSEPH G. ROSA

University of Oklahoma Press
Norman

To the late Bernal ("Bert") Cantwell,

United States Marshal, District of
Kansas (1977-1981), and twice
Colonel of the Kansas Highway Patrol.

In 1980, Bert had me sworn in
before a Federal Judge as a
Special Deputy U. S. Marshal—a rare honor.
Bert shared my avid interest in the
American West and would have enjoyed this book.

Library of Congress Cataloging-in-Publication Data

Rosa, Joseph G.
     Wild Bill Hickok, gunfighter : an account of Hickok's gunfights / by Joseph G. Rosa.
p. cm.
Originally published: College Station, TX : Early West Creative Pub., 2001.
Includes bibliographical references and index.
ISBN 0-8061-3535-2 (alk. paper)
1. Hickok, Wild Bill, 1837–1876. 2. Peace officers —West (U.S.)—Biography. 3. Frontier and
pioneer life—West (U.S.) 4. Violence—West (U.S.)—History—19th century. 5. Firearms—
West (U.S.)—History—19th century. 6. West (U.S.)—Biography. I. Title.
F594.H62 R677 2003
        978'.02–dc21   2002043183

The paper in this book meets the guidelines for permanence and durability of the Committee
on Production Guidelines for Book Longevity of the Council on Library Resources, Inc.

1 2 3 4 5 6 7 8 9 10

Also by Joseph G. Rosa

They Called Him Wild Bill: The Life and Adventures of James Butler Hickok (Norman, 1964, 1974)

Alias Jack McCall (Kansas City, Mo., 1967)

The Gunfighter: Man or Myth? (Norman, 1969)

(with Robin May) *The Pleasure of Guns* (London, 1974)

Colonel Colt London (London, 1976)

Gunsmoke: A Study of Violence in the Wild West (London, 1977), published in the United States as *Gun Law: A Study of Violence in the Wild West* (Chicago, 1977)

Cowboy: The Man and the Myth (London, 1980)

The West of Wild Bill Hickok (Norman, 1982)

Guns of the American West (London, 1985)

Colt Revolvers and the Tower of London (London, 1988)

Buffalo Bill and His Wild West (Lawrence, Kans., 1989)

(with Waldo E. Koop) *Rowdy Joe Lowe: Gambler with a Gun* (Norman, 1989)

Age of the Gunfighter (London, 1993)

(with William C. Davis) *The West* (London, 1994)

Wild Bill Hickok: The Man and His Myth (Lawrence, Kans., 1996)

JOSEPH G. ROSA
The Author

Joseph G. Rosa has had a lifelong affinity with the American West. As an Englishman, the closest he ever imagined he would get to the subject was via the countless "B" Westerns he and his generation watched at every opportunity. But in adulthood, the factual West took over and the lure of the cowboy was overtaken by the exploits of gunfighters and lawmen, in particular Wild Bill Hickok.

Following several years of "airmail research" (an estimated three thousand letters crossed the Atlantic) he published his first book on Hickok, *They Called Him Wild Bill,* in 1964, which was well received both by critics and surviving members of the Hickok family, with whom he formed a close bond.

The Hickok book was followed by *The Gunfighter: Man or Myth?* in 1969; a revised version of *They Called Him Wild Bill* in 1974, and several books on the guns used in the Old West. His analysis of the Hickok legend *Wild Bill Hickok: The Man and the Myth* was published in 1996.

In 1992 Rosa was elected the first non-American President of Westerners International and is the current President of the English Westerners' Society.

CONTENTS

PREFACE

Having written three books about James Butler Hickok (his biography, *They Called Him Wild Bill;* a pictorial history, *The West of Wild Bill Hickok,* and an analysis of his legend, *Wild Bill Hickok: The Man and His Myth),* I assumed that apart from specific articles devoted to blank periods in Hickok's life and a continuing interest in his photographs, there was little else that I could contribute. So when Jim Earle asked me to write a short illustrated book about Wild Bill's gunfights and the guns he used, I leapt at the chance. I was encouraged by news that an "Early West" survey revealed that Hickok was the readers' favorite gunfighter "by a margin of two to one over Billy the Kid, and four to one over John Wesley Hardin."

This is important because despite some revisionist "New West" historians who use "political correctness"—the stealthy manipulation and distortion of historical fact to conform with trendy ideas that judge nineteenth century characters by present day standards—most people prefer Wild Bill Hickok's popular image as a Western two-gun "civilizer" who protected ordinary folk and terrorized "evildoers," familiar to his own and later generations. Understandably, his detractors complain that this image is distorted and make the point that Hickok and other gun-toting individuals impeded rather than promoted the march of civilization. Some did, and it is true that the United States Army and the migration west of thousands of people (aided after the Civil War by the transcontinental railroads) brought so-called civilization to the wilderness rather than gunfighters. But it was Hickok and others who were "in the right place at the right time" placing themselves at risk in tackling lawless individuals, who prepared the way forward—a view current at the time. Writing in the *Leavenworth Daily Commercial* on August 3, 1869, following a vitriolic attack upon Hays City, its inhabitants (including Wild Bill) and the officers at Fort Hays by one E. W. Halford of the Indianapolis *Journal*, "Stoneface" (believed to be Michael E. Joyce) made a spirited response to Halford's allegation that the frontier population was uncivilized, murderous, and "virtuous women" a great rarity:

"Civilization brought Christianity, morality, all that kind of thing 'you know,' and sent the rougher chap to the front. Here we stay and fight and suffer until schools and churches are built, and we get somebody else to assume the responsibility of correcting the 'ill which flesh is heir to.' We build our forts, we sleep upon our arms, and are at all times ready to save the scalp of just such low flung ink slingers as Mr. Halford . . . Time will relieve us of all these evils, as it has many other frontier towns . . ."

Wild Bill's contribution to law and order in Kansas was widely acknowledged in his own lifetime, and many people honestly believed that "no man living could draw and shoot as quickly and accurately" as he could. But in objective hindsight, no-one will ever know who was the "quickest on the draw" or the "deadliest shot" and other feats attributed to so-called "gunfighters." Nonetheless, the real and imaginary six-shooter exploits of Wild Bill and others during the transformation of a wilderness into the United States contributed toward western folklore, and enhanced not only his own reputation, but inspired a worldwide interest in such characters.

Though the real Hickok remains controversial, many historians now acknowledge that the legendary "Wild Bill" personified the public's image of a gunfighter. Huge in stature, broad shouldered, narrow waisted, and graceful in manner and movement, he was a commanding figure. Charismatic and Cavalier-like, he wore his auburn hair shoulder length, and sported a straw-colored mustache. But his blue-gray eyes were his dominant feature. Normally frank and friendly, they became hypnotic and piercing when he was aroused.

The real Wild Bill Hickok may not have killed "considerably over a hundred men," or become "the greatest pistol shot that ever lived," but in the Frontier West, where target accuracy took second place to survival, by pitting his nerve and pistol skill against others in the game of "life or death" he proved himself exceptional, and remains a Frontier Icon.

Joseph G. Rosa
Ruislip, Middlesex,
England

ACKNOWLEDGMENTS

It would not be an exaggeration to say that my debt to various individuals and institutions for help and guidance in preparing this book goes back more than forty years. Sadly, some of those people are now dead; but were aware that they had been acknowledged in my previous books. In reiterating my gratitude to some of those "old-timers" I should also like to thank the following who have been of assistance with this present volume.

The D. L. Becker Family; Vince Bergdale, a dedicated Wild Bill reenactor who depicted Hickok's *modus operandi* with pistols for this book; Delbert Bishop; John Bradbury, Jr.; Lawrence Brooker; Doreen Chaky; David Dary; Terri L. Davis, Director of the Deadwood Public Library; James D. Drees who shared with me his research into early days of Hays City; Diana Duff, the National Archives, Kansas City, Mo.; Paul Fees, Curator, the Buffalo Bill Museum, Cody, Wyoming; R. Sterling Fenn; Robert H. Gibbons; the late Edith Harmon; the late Ethel Hickok; Terry ("Rattlesnake Jake") Hopkins; James S. Hutchins; the late Ida Ipe; James Joplin; Colleen Kirby, Librarian, South Dakota State Historical Society; Mary Kopco, Director, The Adams Museum, Deadwood, SD; Robert Knecht, Manuscripts Division, Kansas State Historical Society; Bob Lee; Greg Martin; Robert ("Bob") McCubbin; Roger McGrath; James D. McLaird; Morgan A. Thomas; Jessica Nashold; Robert Neumann, Curator of the Greene County Archive, Springfield, Mo.; Paul Pixley; James Potter, Historian, John Carter, Photographic Collection, and Robert C. Pettit, Curator, Museum Collections, Nebraska State Historical Society; Sandra Sagala; William B. Secrest; Greg Simpson; Joseph Snell; A. W. F. Taylerson; Thad Turner; R. Larry Wilson, and the Wyoming State Archive. And my sincere apologies to anyone I may have inadvertently neglected to mention.

Joe Rosa

N. C. Wyeth's large pencil sketch of Wild Bill shows him as a "two gun" town-taming marshal. (Courtesy the Adams Museum, Deadwood, South Dakota.)

Chapter One

THE MAKING OF A GUNFIGHTER

James Butler Hickok, generally called "Wild Bill," epitomized the archetypal gunfighter, that half-man, half-myth that became the heir to the mystique of the duelist when that method of resolving differences waned. Indeed, it could be argued that the catalyst for "gunfighting" was the invention of the multiple-shot pistol and the general practice of carrying the revolver as a device of self-protection. A vast number of frontiersmen carried guns mainly because they carried everything they owned on their person and in their saddlebags. Few had homes or roots. Easy access to a gun and whiskey coupled with gambling was the cause of most gunfights—few of which bore any resemblance to the gentlemanly duel of earlier times.

This book is devoted to the analysis of the gunfights of Wild Bill Hickok, the premier gunfighter, whose name comes to mind first when historians and "Wild West" fans discuss guns and gunfighting. They also note that Hickok's gunfights were unusual in that most of them were "fair" fights, not just killings resulting from rage, jealousy over a woman, or drunkenness. And, the majority of his encounters were in his role as lawman or as an individual upholding the law.

It is small wonder that Hickok, whose skill with a pistol was described by some of his contemporaries as "miraculous" and his reflexes "phenomenal," should dominate that breed of man we call *gunfighters.* Understandably, such adulation aroused skepticism among some of his contemporaries, and it must be admitted that Hickok, himself, a great leg-puller, contributed to those tall tales, little realizing, perhaps, that his tongue-in-cheek claim to have killed "considerably over a hundred" men might have inspired his awesome reputation as a "man-killer."

Disregarding men he may have killed during the Civil War, several hostile Indians in 1867, and combatants in publicized gunfights, Hickok's actual "tally" was considerably less than the quoted figure—a fact ignored by most border journalists and others anxious to perpetuate the myth. It was left to Hickok himself to set the record straight. Following a widely circulated report of his death early in 1873, Wild Bill declared it premature, and reacted angrily to the claim that he was a "red-handed murderer" by stating, "If you knew what a wholesome regard I have for damn liars and rascals they would be liable to keep out of my way."[1]

Despite the myths, lies and exaggeration of many of his contemporaries, the real James Butler Hickok did lead the kind of existence that inspired his reputation as a larger than life frontiersman.

*　　　　*　　　　*

The following is a brief chronology of the life of J.B. Hickok.

1837: He was born on May 27, at Homer, La Salle County, Illinois (in later years the name was changed to Troy Grove when it was discovered that another and earlier Homer existed in the northern part of the state). Baptized James Butler Hickok after his mother's father, he was the fifth of seven children born to William Alonzo and Polly Butler Hickok, one brother died in infancy, but four boys and two girls survived. While still in his teens, young James became aware of the antislavery feeling that prevailed in Illinois, and on occasion joined his abolitionist father and some neighbors in rescuing escaped slaves from bounty hunters.

1852: William Alonzo died on May 5, and by 1856 James was anxious to head West, as had his elder brother Oliver (to California) in 1851.

1856: In June, accompanied by his brother Lorenzo, James set off for the newly created territory of Kansas where the brothers hoped to locate some prime farming land. Lorenzo soon returned to Illinois leaving James to explore the area on his own.

1858: Unsuccessful in his search for land in the Leavenworth area,

Wild Bill's birth place photographed in the 1920s shortly before it was torn down and replaced in 1930 by a granite monument and small park dedicated by the State of Illinois. (Author's collection.)

James soon established himself in Monticello township in Johnson County, where, on March 22, he was one of four constables elected to serve the local magistrates. Hickok settled on some land that he hoped to purchase, but learned that a Wyandot Indian had prior claim, so he decided to see more of the West, and he hired on as a teamster for Jones and Cartwright, with whom he remained until April 1861.[2]

1861: Late in April or sometime in May, Hickok appeared at Rock Creek, Nebraska Territory. Two months later he was involved in the so-called "Rock Creek Massacre" that

was to change the whole course of his life.

1861-65: During the Civil War, James Hickok (generally called "Bill" or "William," by which names he had been known since the mid 1850's) served the Union as a wagonmaster, courier, provost marshal's detective and as a scout. It was in this latter capacity, he was to earn the name "Wild Bill" as well as the princely sum of $5 a day (soldiers were paid $13 per month!), and his reputation as a scout and spy. General John B. Sanborn, in command of the District of Southwest Missouri, headquartered at Springfield, had personally

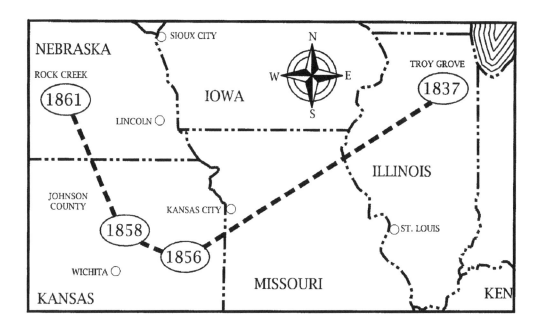

Born in 1837, Hickok migrated to Kansas in 1856, became a constable of Johnson County in 1858, went to Rock Creek, Nebraska in 1861, and became involved in his most famous fight.

appointed him to his staff. Sanborn was to declare in later years that Hickok was the best man he had.

1865: Wild Bill remained in Springfield when the war ended. There he and his friend Davis K. Tutt, a former Confederate soldier, fell out over a card game leading to a gunfight on July 21 that neither man wanted. Charged with murder, later reduced to manslaughter, Hickok was put on trial. His plea of self-defense was accepted by the jury and he was acquitted. Late in September following an unsuccessful attempt to become city marshal of Springfield, Hickok met and was interviewed by Colonel George Ward Nichols, a distinguished former Federal officer who was a writer for *Harper's New Monthly Magazine*. Nichols promised to publish some of "Wild Bill's" adventures.

1866: Late in January or early February, Hickok was ordered to Fort Riley, Kansas, by his former quartermaster Richard Bentley Owen, who had recently been promoted to Assistant Post Quartermaster. On his arrival Hickok was appointed a "special detective" and paid $125 per month to "hunt up" stolen government property. In May, he was detached from Fort Riley to guide Gen-

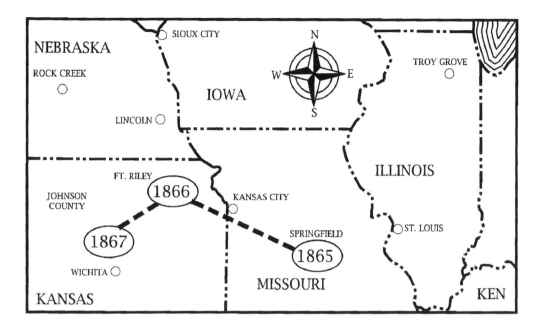

Hickok remained in Springfield at the close of the Civil War in 1865, went to Fort Riley in 1866 as a detective and guide, was later employed as a wagonmaster, and served periodically as a Deputy U.S. Marshal.

eral Sherman and party to Fort Kearny, Nebraska. General John S. Pope then employed him to act as guide on a trip to Santa Fe, New Mexico.[3]

1867: Colonel Nichols honored his promise, and the February issue of *Harper's New Monthly Magazine* carried an article on the exploits of "Wild Bill" which amused, amazed and in some instances infuriated people who knew Hickok intimately. We do not really know what Hickok himself thought of it; but his family recall that he was not pleased. Nevertheless, that story served to publicize "Wild Bill" both nationwide and

internationally, especially in England where *Harper's* enjoyed a limited readership.

1867-69: During that period, Wild Bill was employed as a wagonmaster and later as a scout and courier for the Seventh and Tenth Cavalry regiments. And from August 1867 until early in 1871, he also served intermittently as a Deputy U.S. Marshal in Kansas.[4]

1869: In August Hickok was elected acting sheriff of Ellis County, Kansas, headquartered at Hays City, where his particular method of law enforcement was welcomed. In the

This photograph is believed to have been made at Lawrence in 1858, and is the earliest known image of James Hickok. (Courtesy the late Ethel Hickok.)

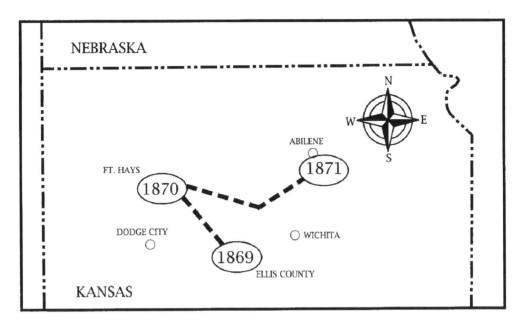

Hickok was elected acting Sheriff of Ellis County, Kansas in 1869, had a shootout with several Seventh Cavalry troopers in Hays City in 1870, and became Marshal of Abilene, Kansas in 1871.

November election, however, his deputy, Peter Lanihan, a Democrat in a largely Democratic community won, and Hickok left office in January 1870.

1870: In March Wild Bill visited old friends in parts of Missouri then resumed his duties as a deputy U. S. Marshal. Perhaps in this capacity he went to Hays City in July where he became involved in a shoot-out with two, possibly more, Seventh Cavalry troopers, killing one and wounding the other.

1871: In early April, Hickok was persuaded to go to Abilene, then the premier shipping point for Texas cattle. On the 15th he accepted the job of marshal or Chief of Police. His predecessor, Thomas James Smith, had been murdered in November of 1870. Known as "Bear River" Tom Smith (a name he earned as a troubleshooter for the Union Pacific Railroad in Wyoming Territory), Smith had proved himself an excellent marshal and was much mourned.

Hickok served as marshal of Abilene for eight months and managed, with the help of several deputies, to keep the Texas cowboys under control. For their part, most of the Texans preferred to keep clear of

The original tintype of this photograph of Wild Bill (circa 1863-64) was probably made either at Springfield or Rolla, Missouri. Reversed to correct the mirror image of the original, Hickok is dressed and armed in his role as a scout or spy. His Colt's Navy revolver is worn butt forward probably for a cross draw. (Courtesy the late Ethel Hickok.)

During eight months in 1873-74, Hickok toured the eastern states shown here as a stage actor with Buffalo Bill's troupe.

Wild Bill for his "man-killer" reputation was well known. Rather, they preferred to face the local gamblers and prostitutes who eagerly fleeced them. By September, however, the council had decided that enough was enough, and ordered Hickok to close down many of the "houses of ill fame" and gambling "hells." By early October few of them remained open, with most of the Texans preparing to return home until the next season.

On October 5, Hickok and Phil Coe, a Texas gambler, clashed and in the ensuing gunfight Coe was fatally wounded and Hickok shot dead another man who ran between them,
gun in hand. This man was Hickok's friend Mike Williams who, during the summer, had been one of the city's jailers.

An attempt upon Hickok's life late in November on a train to Topeka (he successfully foiled it) and a growing animosity toward the cattle trade, prompted the council to meet early in December. Hickok was dismissed as they had no longer any need for his services, and within three months they had also banned the cattle trade.

1872: Wild Bill left Abilene and moved to Kansas City and remained

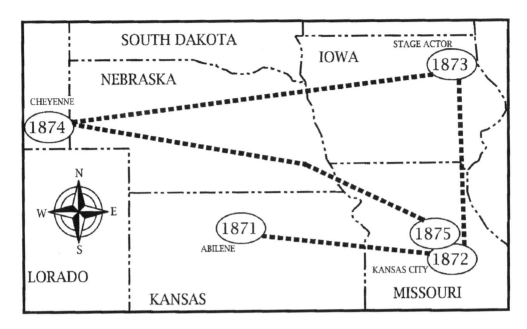

From Abilene, Bill moved to Kansas City in 1872, joined Buffalo Bill's stage show in 1873, moved to Cheyenne in 1874, and returned to Kansas City in 1875.

there off and on through 1875. He eked out an existence as a gambler, with occasional trips as a guide, and the master of ceremonies at a "Grand Buffalo Hunt" at Niagara Falls in August 1872.

1873: In February, it was reported that Wild Bill had been murdered by Texans, which he denied in letters to the press. Starting in September Hickok played himself on stage as a member of Buffalo Bill Cody's theatrical Combination then touring the Eastern states.

1874: By March, however, Hickok, bored with acting, returned West to Kansas City. From there he

moved to Cheyenne, Wyoming Territory, but later moved back to Kansas City and St. Louis, Missouri, where he continued gambling for a living.

1875-76: Wild Bill was no longer interested in law enforcement or scouting for the cavalry, but was still interested in seeing what lay over the hill. In this instance the Black Hills of Dakota Territory. It is clear from the St. Louis press that prior to his trip to Deadwood, Hickok had already spent some time in the Hills.

1876: On March 5, at Cheyenne, he married Agnes Lake Thatcher, the widow of a circus owner and herself

Famed Civil War artist Alfred Waud based this sketch upon a cartes de visite *photograph by Charles W. Scholten of Springfield, Missouri. Wild Bill's coat, buttoned up right-over-left, was optional at the time, and he wears his Colt's Navy pistol butt forward for a reverse draw. (From **Harper's New Monthly** magazine, Feb. 1867.)*

*This photograph of Wild Bill was made in 1872 by Andrew J. White, 712 Main Street, Kansas City, Missouri. Hickok spent much of his time in Kansas City that year, and in September attended the State Fair where he incurred the wrath of about fifty drunken Texas cowboys who had forced the bandmaster to play "Dixie." Hickok ordered the band to stop playing, and although "more than fifty pistols were presented at William's head . . . he came away unscathed," reported the Topeka **Daily Commonwealth** of September 28, 1872. (Author's Collection.)*

an intrepid performer on the high wire and on horseback. It was the culmination of a five year courtship which began when she and her circus arrived at Abilene in 1871. After a brief honeymoon at St Louis and the bride's home at Cincinnati, Ohio, he left her with relatives, promising to send for her, and returned to Cheyenne.

In April, it was announced that he was organizing an expedition to visit the gold fields; but it was abandoned. Instead, he joined Colorado Charley Utter's expedition to the Black Hills. The party reached Deadwood early in July, where Hickok, by his own account, interspersed prospecting with gambling. It was during one of his gambling bouts that he met his end on August 2, shot in the back of the head by John ("Jack") McCall as he played poker in Number 10 Saloon.

*   *   *

In deciding what qualities or traits go toward the making of a gunfighter

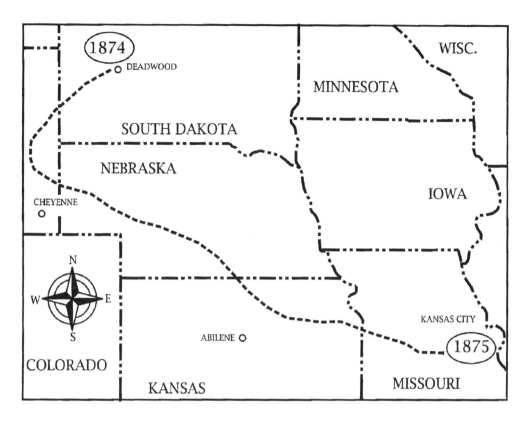

Hickok married Agnes Lake in Cheyenne in 1876, visited her family's home in Cincinnati, returned to Cheyenne, and joined Charlie Utter's expedition to Deadwood, Dakota Territory.

of Hickok's stature, the obvious ability to use a pistol is not by any means the first requirement. Indeed, any person with normal reflexes and either a natural aptitude or the ability to practice toward speed and accuracy in drawing and firing a pistol at a target could be called a "gunfighter."

But speed takes second place to the most important factor which determines whether he will outlive a gunfight—his state of mind. For without the killer instinct, courage and the cold-blooded nerve needed to face down someone who is similarly armed and desperate, even the best shots would find themselves outclassed. Taking one's time to blast away at a paper target with deadly accuracy is fine; but to display such cool and collected deadliness when the target is shooting back with intent to kill, is something else.

In my privileged position as a Special Deputy U.S. Marshal, I was able to talk to a number of professional marshals, and learn something of their attitude toward gun-fights and gunfighters. None of them had much time for "fast draw" fanat-ics. Few of them, the marshals said, had ever been in a kill or be killed situation or experienced the impact of a bullet slamming into bone or vi-tal organs, or suffered the after shock. Thus blinkered, they assume that speed is the essence in a gun-fight rather than an integral part of one's reaction in a life or death con-frontation. The marshals were also anxious to stress that in today's world, legal restraint and a logical assessment of the situation was es-sential before anyone thought of drawing a pistol. They pointed out the wide gulf between how old-time peace officers reacted and the mod-ern approach. Old-timers' reactions depended a lot on circumstances and a reliance upon experience.

For many of them a positive re-action to someone who refused to dis-arm or was determined to kill, was usually backed by local ordinances or state laws. Today, however, law en-forcement officers, U.S. Marshals and others, are bound by certain "pro-cedures" that have to be followed even when faced by a potentially life-threatening situation. Sometimes this gives the "bad guys" an edge, but there are also occasions when cold-blooded courage rather than a justi-fied trigger reaction can save lives.

One deputy marshal, faced by a 16 year-old youth, high on drugs and armed with a .357 Magnum revolver, could justifiably have shot him when he refused to disarm. But he hesi-tated when both realized that they knew each other. The youngster al-lowed the marshal to get close and to talk to him. The marshal's descrip-tion of how they stood face-to-face, the revolver only inches from his stomach, as he distracted him long enough to slide his hand along the barrel and jam it under the hammer just as he pulled the trigger, was chilling. Seeing the look on my face, he grinned and said: "Sure, I was ter-rified, but I could not let him see that. My hand hurt like hell afterwards, but I was more concerned about a change of underwear!"

Back in the Old West, those who assume that the more men he killed, the greater a man's status as a "gun-fighter" are mistaken. Real or imagi-nary "notches" on the butt of a six-shooter proved nothing. What really counted was a man's actions when the chips were down and his reason for killing another person. Wild Bill's authenticated "tally" is less than ten, whereas John Wesley Hardin's (if we believe his claims) is closer to forty—but how many of those killings were fair fights or ambushes only he would know. For when one examines avail-able information about his killings,

Wild Bill as a man about town during his short period with Buffalo Bill's Theatrical Combination in 1873-1874. From a photograph by Gurney and Son of New York. (Author's collection.)

one is left with the impression that Mr. Hardin was more homicidal than humanitarian in his dealings with his fellow man. Hickok on the other hand, while admitting that he had killed a number of men (and ignoring his leg-pulling), was concerned about his press-inspired reputation as a "red-handed murderer." His deep regret over the killing of Mike Williams and his decision to pay for his funeral show a sense of compassion that is not normally expected of a "gunfighter."

This human side of Hickok surprised people who met him face-to-face and knew him only by reputation. In place of the "blustering bully" they found him to be a pleasant, soft-spoken, courteous and worldly individual, whose generosity to others was a byword. This trait impressed John S. Park, who later became a deputy U. S. Marshal at Hays City. In the Lawrence, *Kansas State Journal* of March 5, 1868, he described some of the men who had achieved fame or infamy on the frontier. Hickok he said was just the sort of man who would be expected to perform many of the "daring deeds" attributed to him for which he had won the gratitude and admiration of military commanders under whom he had worked.

Noting that Hickok was regarded in some quarters as a "desperado" Park declared: "I found the report false. I was introduced to him, and received with a hearty shake of the hand, such as does the heart good; none of your touching of two fingers, or gentle pressure of thumb and finger, but a grasping of the whole hand, a regular squeeze, and good, old-fashioned western shake of the arm. Quiet and gentlemanly in his conduct, and appearance; he is well respected by all who are really acquainted with him. While he still possesses the nerve to perform those same deeds again, if required, and the muscle to back him up, he is not quarrelsome as has been represented, but as far as I can learn, peaceably inclined, A true friend to his friends, but a bold enemy to his enemies."

Park's assessment of Wild Bill reiterates the long held belief that when carrying out an official duty, or defending a friend or someone too weak or afraid to stand up for himself, Wild Bill did not think twice about intervening. His oft quoted comment: "I will not be put upon" also included his friends, for he regarded a person's rights as paramount. That he sometimes overstepped the mark (as he did at Abilene by carrying over his shoulder an absentee councilman), prompted the charge that he was "overbearing."

Perhaps, but such actions were a part of Wild Bill's strength of character. And it was this streak of obstinacy that may have contributed to his death. Rather than succumb to alleged threats from men who resented his reputation and his appearance at Deadwood, Hickok dared them to face him. Predictably, it was not an individual brave enough to do so face-to-face, but a back-shooting coward that finally ended the career of the West's most famous pistoleer.

In death, he was immortailized as "Wild Bill Hickok," and his status as the most prominent of Western gunfighters is one of the most enduring of the Old West's many legends, and one that continues to fascinate people of all ages worldwide.

Notes

1. Mendota, Illinois, *Bulletin*, April 11, 1873.

2. Jones & Cartwright to Horace Hickok, June 6, 1861, author's collection.

3. Records of the Quartermaster General (1861-66), National Archives, Washington, D.C.; John B. Sanborn, *The Campaign in Missouri in September And October, 1864*. No place, no date (1890s?). Copy supplied by the University of Missouri, Rolla. The records of Fort Riley disclose that Hickok was absent from the Post from May until September, 1866, and was owed some back pay.

4. Joseph G. Rosa, "J. B. Hickok, Deputy U.S. Marshal." *Kansas History: A Journal of the Central Plains* 2:4 (Winter 1979); most of the records relative to Hickok's service as a deputy are held by the National Archives—Central Plains Region, Kansas City, Missouri.

Chapter Two

WILD BILL'S GUNS

During the past forty years I have been advised of perhaps a half dozen or more guns alleged to have been owned or used by Wild Bill Hickok, including one in the possession of his immediate family. In 1965, his nephew, the late Horace Hickok, allowed me to examine a Colt's Navy revolver which he believed had once belonged to his "uncle Jim." His sister Ethel, however, assured me that it had been purchased during the Civil War by James's brother Lorenzo, and to prove it, showed me letters from him written during the war in which he mentioned sending the pistol home for safekeeping.

In the early 1980's I learned of the existence of a Colt's Navy pistol that was also alleged to have belonged to Wild Bill. Believed to be one of a pair that became separated at his death, it was on loan to the Buffalo Bill Museum Collection at Cody,

Wyoming. Later I was advised that a similar pistol thought to be its "mate" had been discovered in private hands. The serial number of the pistol in the Cody Museum is 204672E, and the other one is numbered 204685E (the "E" was a Colt company definition for extra effort with the engraving and finish). Although thirteen numbers apart, both pistols would be classified as a "matched pair" in that the engraving is similar, and their approximate date of manufacture is 1868. There is one marked difference: the pistol at Cody has a blade foresight (possibly a replacement), whereas its "mate" is fitted with the standard brass pin or bead foresight. The second revolver was purchased in Bloomington, Minnesota, in 1982, from an old man who said that he had lived in South Dakota in earlier years and had obtained his pistol from a

In 1965, Horace Hickok, nephew of Wild Bill, allowed me to handle this Colt's Navy pistol (Serial number 143098) and holster which he said was once owned by his uncle James. His sister Ethel, however, said that it was Lorenzo's pistol. It was manufactured circa 1863. (Author's photograph.)

man who had been around in 1876.[1]

It is reported that both pistols were raffled off after Hickok's death. The late Raymond W. Thorp, however, advised me in the 1950s that the two pistols were actually Colt's 1860 Model Armies. Fortunately, he provided the serial number of one of the weapons, 204672, the same number as the weapon at Cody. He further advised that the man who won the pistol was William Burroughs. Mr. Burroughs in turn passed it down in the family to I. M. Jenkins who later loaned it to the Buffalo Bill Museum at Cody. Obviously, Thorp's information concerning the Model was incorrect; but even allowing for that, the provenance of both pistols

is more hearsay than fact. The most famous of the reported Wild Bill pistols, however, actually bears his name on the backstrap and has an interesting if flawed provenance.

During the early 1950s, the Texas Gun Collectors Association magazine published a montage photograph of an engraved ivory-handled Colt's Old Model Navy pistol that depicted the backstrap inscription "J. B. HICKOCK 1869." By the time that I became aware of that photograph, it had appeared in print elsewhere and was reported to be one of a pair of Navy pistols presented to Hickok in 1869 by the Union Pacific Railway Company (Eastern Division) for "cleaning up

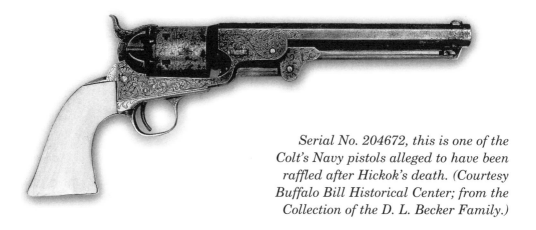

Serial No. 204672, this is one of the Colt's Navy pistols alleged to have been raffled after Hickok's death. (Courtesy Buffalo Bill Historical Center; from the Collection of the D. L. Becker Family.)

A left side view of the same pistol (SN 204672). (Courtesy Buffalo Bill Historical Center; from the Collection of the D. L. Becker Family.)

Hays City, Kansas." In 1881, J. W. Buel in his book, *Heroes of the Plains*, claimed that a pair of pistols were the gift from Senator Henry Wilson and friends to show their appreciation of Hickok's services as a guide on the plains in 1869. The Wilson trip never took place, and there is no evidence that the U.P.E.D. (which became the Kansas Pacific Railway in March 1869) ever presented Hickok with a pair of pistols.

There the trail ran cold until 1975 when I learned that the pistol had resurfaced. It had been offered to the Buffalo Bill Museum at Cody who turned it down because the backstrap inscription had been altered. Subsequent correspondence on my part with the then owner, led to a meeting in London where it was revealed that it had been in a bank vault since 1937 following exhibition in Chicago to publicize Gary Cooper's

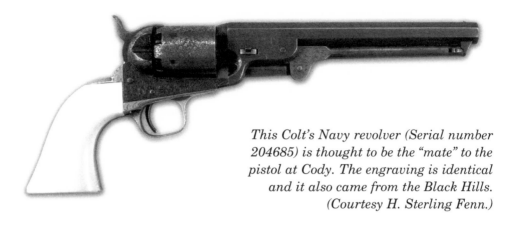

This Colt's Navy revolver (Serial number 204685) is thought to be the "mate" to the pistol at Cody. The engraving is identical and it also came from the Black Hills. (Courtesy H. Sterling Fenn.)

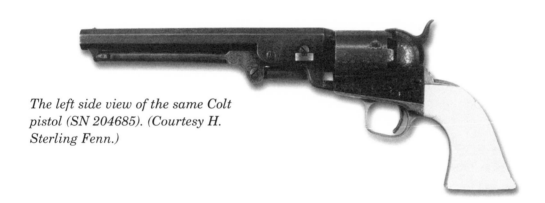

The left side view of the same Colt pistol (SN 204685). (Courtesy H. Sterling Fenn.)

portrayal of Hickok in the movie, *The Plainsman*. My immediate concern, of course, was to learn who had changed the inscription from HICKOCK to HICKOK.

Larry Wilson, the foremost Colt pistol expert, who later minutely examined the pistol, told me that only by running a finger along the lettering was it possible to detect a slight bump, for it was expertly changed. The name J. B. Hickok is written in pencil inside the ivory grips, and it is accompanied by its original lined, leather holster which has the initials "J.B.H." inked inside.

It was suggested that perhaps the original engraver realized his mistake in misspelling Hickok and corrected it, but I tactfully pointed out that he would have been more than a century old at the time! I reexamined the original photograph on file at the Connecticut State Library

This Colt's Navy serial numbered 138813 (the cylinder is numbered thirteen digits apart from the rest of the gun) is reputed to have been owned by Wild Bill. Photographed circa 1936-37, it clearly shows the misspelling of Hickok as "Hickock" on the backstrap. (Photographed by Raymond M. Stagg. Courtesy the Connecticut State Library.)

which was credited to "STAGG-LA 762 S. Garland." Some protracted research into various photographers named "Stagg" from the Los Angeles area (two of whom served in the United States Navy in similar capacities during World War II) finally led me to the original photographer—Raymond M. Stagg who was listed at that address until 1937. This suggests that the photograph was part of the publicity for the film. Evidently, a print was sent to the Colt Company for reference or, perhaps, in the hope that they could find the pistol in their records. The pistol, serial numbered 138813, was manu-

factured circa 1864. Unfortunately, following a serious fire that year, Colt's records are incomplete and they were unable to find any trace of it. One interesting fact has emerged however, the cylinder is numbered thirteen digits apart from the rest of the pistol which suggests that it was once one of a pair (curiously, the previously mentioned Navy at Cody and its "mate" are also thirteen digits apart!). Therefore, should a second pistol turn up, bearing the original misspelled inscription, and a mismatched cylinder, it would boost the claim that the pistols were once owned by Hickok. But even assum-

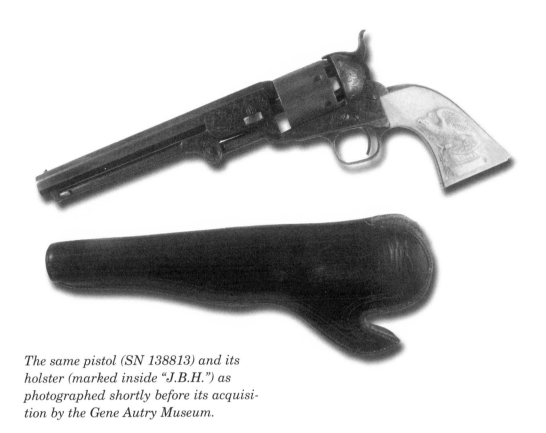

The same pistol (SN 138813) and its holster (marked inside "J.B.H.") as photographed shortly before its acquisition by the Gene Autry Museum.

The changed inscription from HICKOCK to HICKOK is clear. Hickok's name also appears on the inside of the ivory grips. (Photographs courtesy of Greg Martin.)

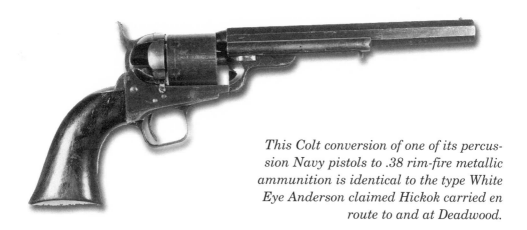

This Colt conversion of one of its percussion Navy pistols to .38 rim-fire metallic ammunition is identical to the type White Eye Anderson claimed Hickok carried en route to and at Deadwood.

ing that the pistol(s) is genuine, its provenance does not inspire confidence.

Hickok carried a pair (or pairs) of standard walnut-stocked Navy pistols until circa 1866-67. But by April 1867, Henry M. Stanley reported that Wild Bill's armament was a pair of silver mounted ivory-handled pistols. Here, it is important to point out that "silver mounted ivory-handled" does not necessarily mean that the frame, barrel and mountings were also florally engraved. It usually meant that the normally plain brass trigger-guard and backstrap had been plated and the grips made from ivory instead of the usual walnut. Photographs made in 1867 and 1869 which depict Hickok wearing those pistols are not clear enough to suggest any floral engraving. So the question is: did he possess more than one pair of ivory-handled Navies—the second pair being the engraved "1869" presentation?

The owner of the alleged surviving pistol (SN 138813) when I became involved in 1975, was the daughter of Harry Marietta, a direct descen-

Wild Bill, armed with a pair of Colt's Navy pistols worn for the plains- or reverse- draw and a Bowie-type butcher knife in his belt. Some historians have concluded that this plate was made during his period with Cody in 1873-74. The original cartes de visite *is credited to Wilbur Blakeslee of Mendota, Illinois. Hickok was there in March 1869 and a close examination of the photograph reveals that he wears his hair parted in the middle, an affectation he had discarded by 1870. This image shows him as he was remembered by Adolph Roenigk who saw him similarly dressed in 1869. (Courtesy the Kansas State Historical Society.)*

"Scouts of the Plains." Left to right: Elisha Green, Wild Bill, Buffalo Bill Cody, Texas Jack Omohundro, and Eugene Overton, photographed circa 1873-74. Hickok and Green are armed with studio prop rifles, but the remaining weapons are those used on stage. (Courtesy the Denver Public Library, Western History Collection.)

dant of the founders of Marietta, Ohio. Born in the 1890's, by the early years of this century he was a prosperous land surveyor in Chicago. His "Western" interests in ranching and firearms, however, were lifelong, and he also patronized the Buffalo Bill Museum at Cody, Wyoming, and was a friend of many of the surviving old-timers. He also owned a Colt's revolver described as a ".44 caliber, No. 50679" once owned by Buffalo Bill,

which he loaned to the Cody museum for exhibition in 1931. The Buffalo Bill Museum records have revealed that the pistol was a .44-40 Frontier Six-Shooter.

In 1932 Mr. Marietta began corresponding with Maurice C. Clark of Los Angeles, a gun dealer, who sold him a small Belgian-made .30 caliber "Deringer-type" pistol that he claimed had been taken from the body of Joseph Alfred ("Jack") Slade,

This portion is all that exists of a large format tintype of the foregoing plate, and provides a close up of Hickok and his pistol butt that appears to have a lanyard ring set in the lower butt flat. (Courtesy the Smithsonian Institution.)

the "Terror of the Overland Stage" when he was hanged by vigilantes at Virginia City, Montana, on March 10, 1864. The hangman, John Xavier Beidler—generally known as "X" Beidler—had taken the pistol. He later told Clark's father that Slade had worn the pistol on his watch chain. Beidler himself "wore it for approximately 20 years on a huge gold watch chain across his vest front." Clark's father purchased the pistol from him and continued the tradition as did M.C. Clark.

Following Beidler's death in 1890, Clark's father also purchased from his family a Colt's Navy pistol alleged to have been once owned by Wild Bill Hickok. Clark informed Mr. Marietta that Hickok had carried the pistol with him to Deadwood and, following his death, "it went to his intimate friend J. X. Beidler United States Marshal who officiated at his funeral." He added: "This gun came to my father, W. Guy Clark, for X was a close acquaintance and it has been in our family ever since, or roughly forty years." Clark's father had made a close study of Wild Bill and was convinced that the pistol was one of the pair allegedly presented at Hays City, but that its mate had probably been "lost to mankind for ever."

Harry Marietta purchased the Hickok pistol from Clark in 1932. In 1936, when he learned that Cecile B.

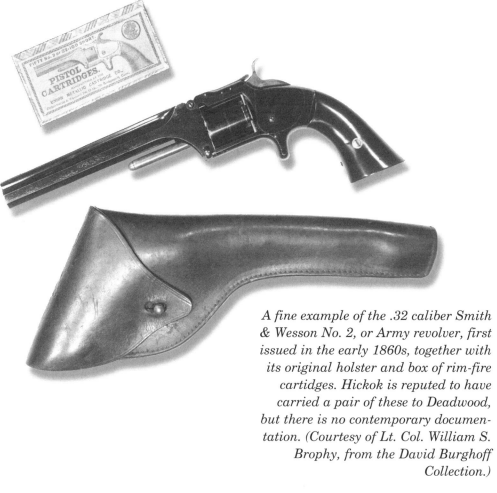

A fine example of the .32 caliber Smith & Wesson No. 2, or Army revolver, first issued in the early 1860s, together with its original holster and box of rim-fire cartridges. Hickok is reputed to have carried a pair of these to Deadwood, but there is no contemporary documentation. (Courtesy of Lt. Col. William S. Brophy, from the David Burghoff Collection.)

DeMille was to film the life of Wild Bill Hickok, he realized that there would be considerable interest in the pistol. Similarly, the Hickok family (with whom he had had some correspondence concerning the pistol) also took an interest. Wild Bill's nephews, Horace A. and his brother Howard L. Hickok, offered DeMille information and photographs to ensure accuracy, DeMille, however, took little notice of their advice or protests when they learned that he planned to feature "Calamity Jane!"

Once DeMille's movie *The Plainsman* was publicized, Harry Marietta was persuaded to loan both the Hickok and Cody pistols to the Balaban and Katz Corporation of Chicago for exhibition at the Tivoli Theater for one week in February 1937. The pistols were returned to their bank vault and remained there until Mr. Marietta's death in 1968. His daughter told me that when her father remarried, a lot of his corre-

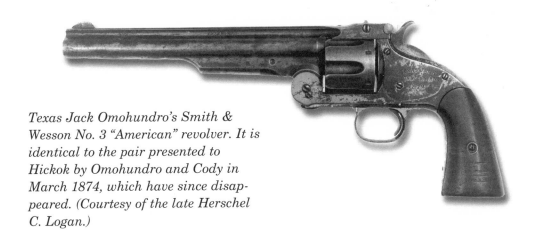

Texas Jack Omohundro's Smith & Wesson No. 3 "American" revolver. It is identical to the pair presented to Hickok by Omohundro and Cody in March 1874, which have since disappeared. (Courtesy of the late Herschel C. Logan.)

spondence and other material authenticating some of the arms in his collection disappeared; but the Hickok pistol and its accompanying documents remained safely locked up in the vault.[2]

When reviewing the material accompanying the pistol I soon realized that some of it was based upon hearsay. Following his vigilante days, X. Beidler was indeed a deputy U.S. Marshal, but was living in Montana when Hickok was killed in Deadwood. Similarly, many historians and researchers were skeptical of historical pieces because of their dubious origins. Consequently, that shared skepticism and the changed backstrap inscription prompted me to doubt the pistol's authenticity when I published my book *The West of Wild Bill Hickok* in 1982. However, if we accept as fact that Beidler did come to possess the pistol or pistols,

it may well be that *his* descendants credited him with being present at Deadwood to add color and credibility to the claim. Therefore, I remain open-minded on the pistol (SN 138813) itself. If its present owners, the Gene Autry Museum of Western Collections, can employ its considerable resources to authenticate the pistol (and, we hope, find its mate), and learn who changed the inscription and when, then they will indeed possess a truly unique relic of Wild Bill.

In attempting to authenticate alleged Hickok-owned pistols based upon accompanying documentation, many writers have ignored contemporary references to Hickok's firearms, preferring instead to accept so-called documentation, and old age and failing memories makes many old-timers' reminiscences suspect. An exception was Joseph F. ("White-

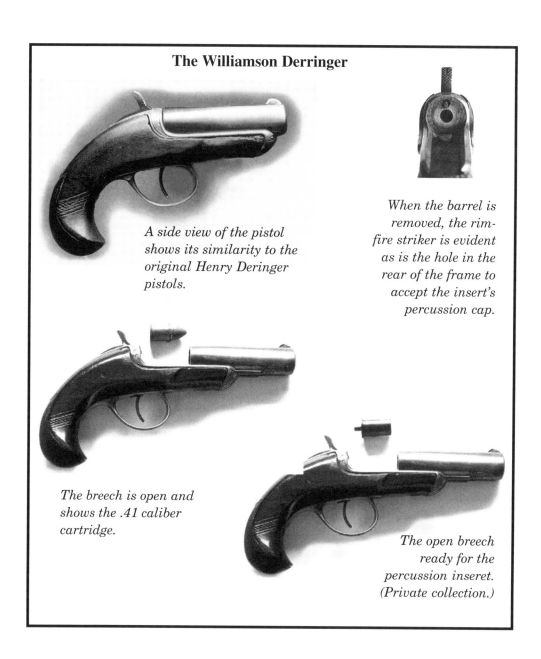

The Williamson Derringer

A side view of the pistol shows its similarity to the original Henry Deringer pistols.

When the barrel is removed, the rim-fire striker is evident as is the hole in the rear of the frame to accept the insert's percussion cap.

The breech is open and shows the .41 caliber cartridge.

The open breech ready for the percussion inseret. (Private collection.)

Eye") Anderson, who accompanied Hickok to Deadwood, and who claimed that Wild Bill was then armed with a pair of Colt's .36 caliber cartridge six-shooters.[3]

These pistols were actually classified as .38 caliber and were either converted percussion Navies or factory made from existing percussion parts. The most common caliber was in .38 rim-fire. Manufactured under the Richards-Mason patents they were produced by Colt as stopgap models pending the introduction of a

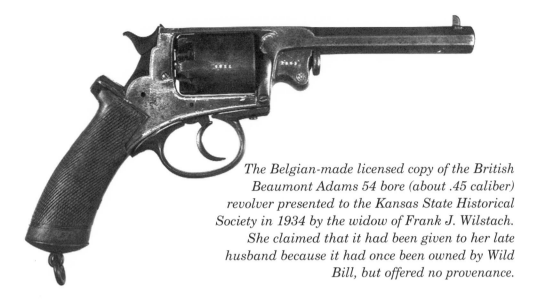

The Belgian-made licensed copy of the British Beaumont Adams 54 bore (about .45 caliber) revolver presented to the Kansas State Historical Society in 1934 by the widow of Frank J. Wilstach. She claimed that it had been given to her late husband because it had once been owned by Wild Bill, but offered no provenance.

new breed of cartridge pistols that culminated in the Single Action Army, Model of 1873 (the "Peacemaker"). Hickok was also known to own a pair of .44 caliber Smith & Wesson Number 3 Army or standard "American" model pistols. The definition "American" was to distinguish the model from a version produced under contract to the Russian government that included a trigger-guard spur, a lanyard butt swivel, and a specially ordered .44 caliber cartridge. The two "American" revolvers were presented to Wild Bill by Buffalo Bill and Texas Jack Omohundro in March 1874 when he left Cody's theatrical Combination to return West.

Add to that list one or a pair of .32 caliber Smith & Wesson Number 2 Army pistols; a Sharps' four-barrel .32 caliber Deringer-type pistol, and the list is impressive Among other weapons besides his Colt's Navy pistols reputed to have been owned or used by Wild Bill during his career were a pair of single shot .41 caliber Williamson dual-ignition Deringers. Missing, of course, is any contemporary reference to the Colt's Peacemaker, despite the later claim by Robert A. Kane, writing in *Outdoor Life* in 1906 that Hickok owned a pair of Colt's .44 caliber Single Action Army pistols, and a pair of Remingtons in the same caliber.[4]

In the 1940s, the family of Captain Jack Crawford exhibited a number of weapons from his collection and alleged to have been owned by famous Westerners. Among these was a .31 caliber Colt's Pocket Pistol, commonly called the Model of

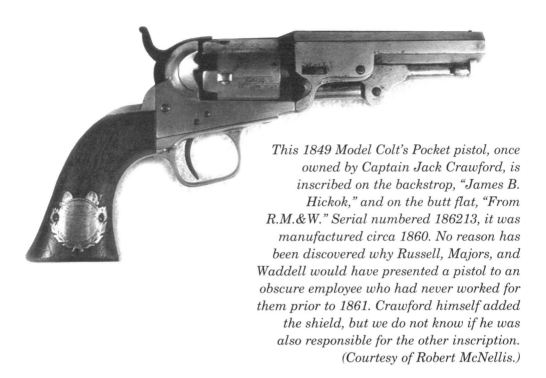

This 1849 Model Colt's Pocket pistol, once owned by Captain Jack Crawford, is inscribed on the backstrop, "James B. Hickok," and on the butt flat, "From R.M.&W." Serial numbered 186213, it was manufactured circa 1860. No reason has been discovered why Russell, Majors, and Waddell would have presented a pistol to an obscure employee who had never worked for them prior to 1861. Crawford himself added the shield, but we do not know if he was also responsible for the other inscription. (Courtesy of Robert McNellis.)

1849. On a silver shield *screwed* to the right side of the stock is the legend: "Wild Bill, to Capt. Jack BLACK HILLS 1876." The backstrap, however, is inscribed: "James B. Hickok," and on the butt flat: "From R. M. & W." Numbered 186213 the pistol dates from circa 1860, but we believe that the inscription suggesting that it was presented by Russell, Majors & Waddell to Hickok following the Rock Creek affair, is questionable for several reasons. Wild Bill's niece Ethel advised this writer that during several visits to Troy Grove (she was present at the time), Jack Crawford bemoaned the fact that he did not own one of Wild Bill's pistols, presumably in the hope they might

give him one! She also provided me with written proof that Hickok worked for the company's rivals, Jones and Cartwright, until two months before the Rock Creek incident. Since RM&W were bankrupt at the time, and Hickok would have been unknown even to Ben Ficklin, the line superintendent, the pistol and its inscriptions must be viewed with skepticism. But when was Hickok's name and the presentation from RM&W added, and by whom?

Early in his career Hickok is reported to have carried a Colt's .44 caliber Dragoon pistol and at various times owned one or a pair of its successor, the Colt's New Model Army pistol of 1860. These together

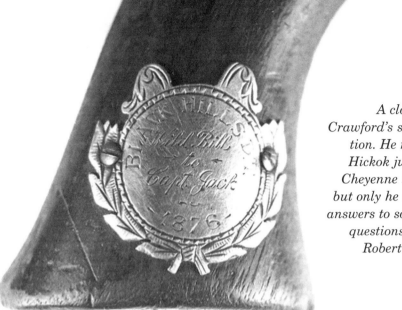

A close-up view of Crawford's shield inscription. He may have met Hickok just the once at Cheyenne in June 1876, but only he could provide answers to some awkward questions, (Courtesy of Robert E. McNellis.)

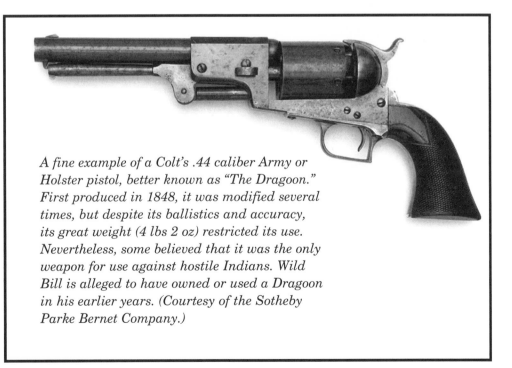

A fine example of a Colt's .44 caliber Army or Holster pistol, better known as "The Dragoon." First produced in 1848, it was modified several times, but despite its ballistics and accuracy, its great weight (4 lbs 2 oz) restricted its use. Nevertheless, some believed that it was the only weapon for use against hostile Indians. Wild Bill is alleged to have owned or used a Dragoon in his earlier years. (Courtesy of the Sotheby Parke Bernet Company.)

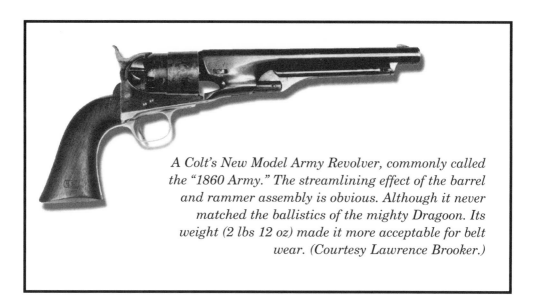

A Colt's New Model Army Revolver, commonly called the "1860 Army." The streamlining effect of the barrel and rammer assembly is obvious. Although it never matched the ballistics of the mighty Dragoon. Its weight (2 lbs 12 oz) made it more acceptable for belt wear. (Courtesy Lawrence Brooker.)

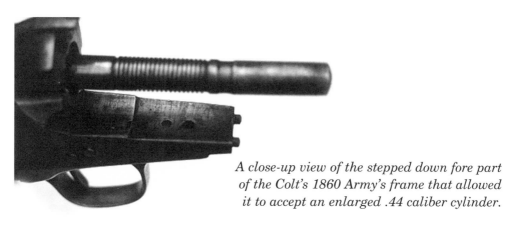

A close-up view of the stepped down fore part of the Colt's 1860 Army's frame that allowed it to accept an enlarged .44 caliber cylinder.

with a pair of round barreled 1861 Colt's Navies and a .44 Model 1866 Winchester rifle, and probably a Spencer carbine and various Sharps' arms all form a part of Hickok's alleged armoury. Unfortunately, there are no other details to prove if and when he owned all or any of them.

Some enthusiastic collectors are prepared to accept the alleged provenance of a gun or artifact as genuine if it cannot be disproved. With the passing of time, however, there is the danger that weapons attributed to individuals (as a joke or with the intention to defraud) become accepted simply because the story is told so many times that it becomes "fact." The best example is the Peacemaker allegedly used by Pat Garrett to kill Billy the Kid in July 1881 which was reported to have been taken from

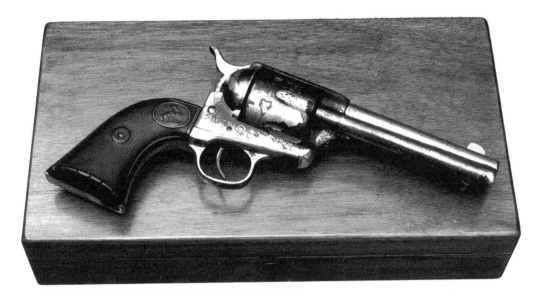

This Colt .45 single action (SN 139345) was accepted by many writers for a time as having belonged to Hickok and Pat Garrett, but it was made in 1891 and could not have been Hickok's gun.

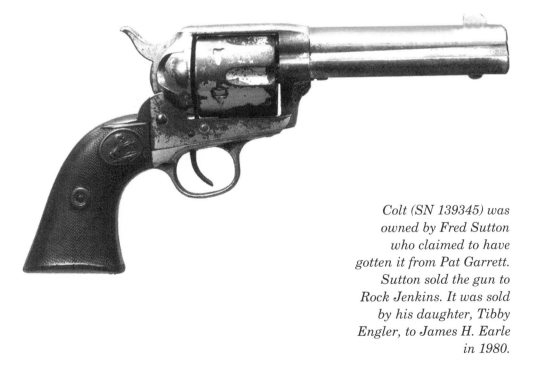

Colt (SN 139345) was owned by Fred Sutton who claimed to have gotten it from Pat Garrett. Sutton sold the gun to Rock Jenkins. It was sold by his daughter, Tibby Engler, to James H. Earle in 1980.

Hickok's body when he was killed.

Serial numbered 139345, the pistol came to light, together with a number of others, in the early years of this century when it was in the hands of Fred Sutton who claimed to have known most of the early day gunfighting lawmen and some of the outlaw fraternity. Among a number of typewritten letters authenticating various weapons was one dated January 12, 1902, addressed to Fred Sutton, supposedly from, Garrett in which it was claimed:

> This morning I met our old friend from Dodge City, Billie Tilghman, and we had a good visit. I am sending you by him the Wild Bill six gun you have wanted so long, the Colts 45 No. 139,345, with the dog filed off, and engraved 'Wild Bill' on the handle. This is the gun that I put your friend Bonny out of business with at the Pete Maxwell Ranch on July 14, 1882 [sic—1881].
>
> Bill had this gun on when Jack McCall killed him, and it was sent to me a short time later by his sister, Mrs. Lydia M. Barnes, of Oberlin, Kansas. I hope I am now done carrying guns, for I feel I have served my time at that . . . Please don't part with this gun and drop me a line upon receipt of it . . .

Lydia Barnes recalled in 1915 that the Hickok family never received any of her brother James' pistols, but that is academic, for the pistol was made too late (fifteen years after Hickok's death) to have belonged to him. When I asked the Colt company in 1957 when single action SN 139345 was made they replied that it was shipped to E. K. Tryon Jr. and Company of Philadelphia, Pennsylvania, on April 14, 1891.[5]

Sutton eventually sold this pistol and a number of others to R. C. Jenkins of Orleans, Indiana, in 1929-30. Curiously, his "To Whom It May Concern" declarations appear to have been typed on the same typewriter that was supposedly used by Garrett and company! The Sutton-Jenkins Collection was on display at the Museum of the Great Plains at Lawton, Oklahoma, before it was dispersed at auction by Sotheby Parke Bernet of Los Angeles on April, 20, 1980. The pistol that Sutton alleged as belonging to Hickok pistol is owned by James H. Earle.

In his classic book, *The Chisholm Trail,* Wayne Gard in describing Hickok's armament noted that when he was dressed up, "his double-action Army pistols gave way to silver-mounted, pearl-handled revolvers." During a conversation with him in 1965, I asked him if he was referring to Colt's double-action Army revolvers which were not manufactured until after Hickok's death, and was he aware that Wild Bill's silver-mounted single-action revolvers had ivory, not pearl grips? I also mentioned that someone once asked General George Patton why he carried revolvers with pearl handles. He is alleged to have replied, "Pearl is for pimps—them's ivory!"

Mr. Gard enjoyed the story, but said that he got his information in Kansas when he was shown the pistol illustrated on page 41, purported to be the sole survivor of the pair of double-action revolvers. It is most unlikely that Hickok knew of its existence.

Historical artifacts alleged to be owned by or associated with famous individuals can only be accepted as genuine when there is sound evidence to prove it. Otherwise they remain as "purported to have been owned or used by" which is the fate of so many reputed Hickok guns. But if Wild Bill's alleged pistols continue to be controversial, as we shall see later on in our story, his rifle certainly was not.

Notes

1. I am indebted to Dr. Paul Fees of the Buffalo Bill Museum at Cody, Wyoming, for allowing me to examine the pistol in the museum's collection and to Mr. H. Sterling Fenn for letting me handle its "mate."

2. In 1975 John Wisner and his wife kindly supplied me with xerox copies of their material relative to this pistol.

3. For the story of Joseph Anderson, see William B. Secrest's *I Buried Hickok*, Creative Publishing Company, College Station, Texas.

4. A review of the alleged Hickok pistols is to be found in *They Called Him Wild Bill* by Joseph G. Rosa.

5. Colt's Patent Fire Arms Manufacturing Company, Hartford, Connecticutt, to Joseph G. Rosa, September 18, 1957.

Chapter Three

THE PISTOLEER

Wild Bill Hickok's favorite weapons, according to an unnamed admirer in the Chicago *Tribune* of August 25, 1876, "were Colt's 'Navies,' and in the rapid and wonderfully accurate use of them, it is admitted he had no equal in the West. They were handsome ivory-handled articles, and were always at that time swinging to his belt."

The same individual also summed up Hickok's attitude toward gunfights: "The secret of Bill's success was his ability to draw and discharge his pistols, with a rapidity that was truly wonderful and a peculiarity of his was that the two were presented and discharged simultaneously, being 'out and off' before the average man had time to think about it. He never seemed to take any aim, yet he never missed.

"Bill never did things by halves. When he drew his pistols it was always to shoot, and it was a theory of his that every man did the same."

Despite a hint of hero-worship, the writer does make the point that Hickok preferred the Navy revolver to all others and that his reaction to a killing situation invariably gave him an advantage. But it does not prove how good a pistol shot he really was. There are numerous accounts of Wild Bill's "miraculous" marksmanship, many of them tall stories, while others ring true, particularly those that have been duplicated by modern experts.

Perhaps the most professional assessment of Wild Bill's alleged skill came from a man who was probably one of the finest "pistoleers" of them all—Ed McGivern. Having grown up

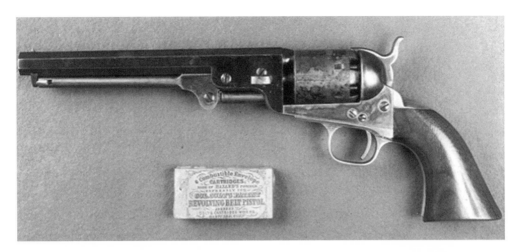

A fine example of the later model Colt's Navy revolver as used during and after the Civil War, togehter with a box of Colt-made combustible cartridges. (Courtesy of Lawrence Brooker.)

with tales of Wild Bill and his ilk, he determined to duplicate as many of their alleged feats as possible. He concluded that "there can be little doubt about his [Hickok's] proficiency with his pistols. He certainly could not have survived all of the gun battles chalked up to his credit if he had not been a more than average expert in the handling of his guns."[1]

Buffalo Bill Cody at various times praised Hickok's marksmanship, and shortly before his death on January 10, 1917, he was interviewed for *Outdoor Life* by Chauncey Thomas, a well known journalist and gun enthusiast. In later years Thomas was reported to have owned some of Hickok's paper targets, but their whereabouts are unknown today.

Cody told Thomas that Hickok's marksmanship was good, but his strength was in his ability to keep cool under fire and not get rattled. Whereas most men would pull their pistols and then cock them, Wild Bill cocked his as they were drawn and fired as they came level. As for Wild Bill's mankiller reputation, Cody remarked that "Bill Hickok was not a bad man, as is so often pictured. But he was a bad man to tackle. Always kinda cheerful, almost about it. And he never killed a man unless that man was trying to kill him. That's fair."

Earlier, interviewed in the Burlington, Iowa, *The Daily Hawk-Eye* of January 29, 1886, Cody declared that he had known Hickok like a brother for twenty years:

He was a man with a whole world of nerve and one of the kindest, best-

The Cross Draw
(Demonstrated
by Vince Bergdale.

1. The hands are at the side.

2. Both arms cross the body and the hands grasp the pistol butts.

3. The hammers are cocked as the pistorls are being drawn.

4. Both pistols are now free.

5. The pistols are fully cocked as they come level.

ness and his certain aim saved him. The other fellow was quietly buried, for none of Bill's subjects ever went away and got cured so they could make him future trouble . . .

Others of course have been less than generous when discussing Hickok's marksmanship and motivation. Some have even compared him with the modern pistol shot (ignoring the great gulf between percussion revolvers and modern precision-made target pistols) and concluded that he and his kind would have been humiliated by the average Olympic marksman.

hearted fellows on earth. He seemed to be unfortunate in getting into scrapes, but he always "got" his man when he went for him. He was not actually responsible for many of his battles, but having killed a few men and acquired a considerable degree of notoriety as a quick man with his pistol and a dead shot, he was sought for and compelled to fight. The country was full of bad men, murderous ruffians who committed reckless deeds, simply for the reputation it gave them. These fellows used to hunt Bill up every time he came into a place and they generally found him when they looked for him. In all the fights he had no one ever succeeded in getting him down. His fatal cool-

Yet another great pistolman, the celebrated Walter Winans (who with Ira Payne was reckoned to be one of the best pistol shots of the late 19th century) declared that target shooting was fine, but it taught one nothing about survival. In effect, the modern Olympic champions who employ what are best described as "scientific instruments" rather than recognizable firearms to perform some remarkable feats, would indeed humiliate the old-time gunfighters when shooting at targets; but few Olympic marksmen would survive a gunfight.[2]

Another facet of nineteenth century and earlier firearms put forward by some skeptics is the alleged problem of smoke when a weapon was discharged. Some writers (many of

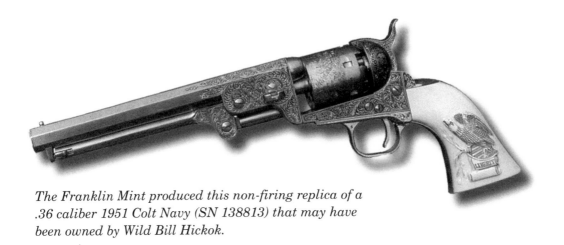

The Franklin Mint produced this non-firing replica of a .36 caliber 1951 Colt Navy (SN 138813) that may have been owned by Wild Bill Hickok.

whom have never fired a weapon of any kind) gleefully claim that the smoke was so dense that it was like firing through a fog. This is nonsense. A discharge of a number of weapons in a confined space, such as a saloon bar, might cause such problems, but not shots fired in the open air where it tended to clear rapidly, for black powder, contrary to some reports produces white, not black or brown smoke.

Hickok's real and imaginary marksmanship has been discussed at length elsewhere,[3] but in summary, stories crediting him with miraculous accuracy with a pistol at distances over two hundred yards, or firing deringers at targets seventy-five yards away have to be treated with caution or discounted. For while we know that he shot Dave Tutt through the chest (who stood sideways in a dueling fashion) with a Navy revolver

at seventy-five yards, most of Hickok's pistol encounters were fought at ranges between eight and twelve feet. As for the deringer stories, many of them owe their origin to J. W. Buel's *Heroes of the Plains* that was published in the 1880s.

Being a "dead shot" with a pistol has long been the principal asset of the Western hero. Colonel George Ward Nichols featured Hickok's skill in his *Harper's* article when he described how he fired at the letter "O" in a sign on a building fifty yards away, first promising Nichols that he would put all six balls "inside of the circle," which he did. Years later, Bat Masterson, Alfred Henry Lewis, and Stuart N. Lake transferred the exhibition to Kansas City, but upped the distance to 100 yards. A good pistol shot can indeed hit such a target, but there is no real proof that Hickok indulged himself or others by such shooting.

The Reverse or Plains Draw
Demonstrated by Vince Bergdale.

1. *The hands are at the side.*

2. *The hands turn inward to grasp the butts while the thumbs hook over the hammers and the index fingers enter the trigger guards*

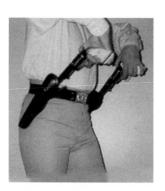

3. *The pistols are on the move out of their holsters.*

4. *Free of their holsters, the pistols are spun upward . . .*

5. *. . . and are cocked. . .*

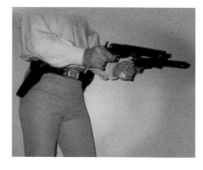

6. *. . . and leveled on their target.*

The Reverse or Plains Draw
Demonstrated by Vince Bergdale.

1. *The hands are at the side.*

2. *The hands grip the guns.*

3. *The pistols are pulled.*

4. *The fingers are placed in the triggerguard as the pistols are moving.*

5. *The guns clear their holsters and are leveled at their target.*

Leander P. Richardson who met Wild Bill the day before he was killed wrote that he saw him toss a tomato can fifteen feet into the air before drawing his pistols and putting two bullets into it before it hit the ground. He then bounced it along the ground with bullets until both pistols were empty. Personal attempts at "plinking" (as most target shooters would call this) proved satisfactory, but I doubt some of the aerial marksmanship credited to single-action shooting at tin cans. Ed McGivern proved that the double-action was best suited to that form of exhibitionism.

Writing in 1912, Robert W. Kane also claimed to have watched Hickok toss a tomato can into the air (thirty feet!) and hit it three times before it struck the ground—twice with his right hand pistol and once with the left. He also described Hickok's simultaneous discharge when standing midway between two telegraph poles 176 feet apart and hitting both of them. He concluded that "I am prepared to believe any story of his skill or prowess that does not conflict with the laws of gravitation and physics."[4]

The ability to use a pistol, even if it was never fired in anger, was an essential part of one's existence during the frontier period of Western expansion. Some men used a pistol to solve all their problems, and invariably paid the price, while others carried and used firearms for self-protection; in pursuance of an official act, or as a deterrent to others which aptly describes Hickok's motivation.

Pistols, like clothing, were an individual preference and in carrying them, some men sometimes displayed odd choices. Some carried their pistols thrust into belts or waistbands, and others in one boot top, and a Bowie knife in the other. During the percussion era, however, most pistols were carried in holsters (sometimes called "scabbards") on a waist belt, and worn butt forward. For those of us brought up on Hollywood Westerns, which invariably depict revolvers thrust into holsters hung from a slit cut into the belt (the so-called "Buscadero" rig), and with the butt to the rear for a conventional hip draw, it comes as a surprise to see photographs of Hickok and his contemporaries wearing their pistols waist high and butts forward. One's immediate reaction is to assume that they used a cross body draw (some did); but far more likely it was for the very popular "Plains" or "Reverse" draw which was common to the frontier, and officially adopted by the United States Army—particularly the cavalry.

Few Western movie stars, however, have featured the reverse draw. Randolph Scott used it on occasion as did Joel McCrea in *Union Pacific*, and later William ("Wild Bill") Elliott and television's Hickok, Guy Madison. But it was Gary Cooper's reverse draw in *The Plainsman* that is best remembered (Cooper also used a reverse draw with a pair of flintlock pistols in the Revolutionary War epic *Unconquered* which was more amusing than dramatic!).

Later, in the early 1950s, when the inferior remake of the classic silent era film *The Pony Express* appeared, it was reported in a British film magazine that Forrest Tucker (who played Hickok to Charlton Heston's Buffalo Bill) was armed with the same pair of pistols used by Cooper in *The Plainsman*. Unfortunately, Mr. Tucker's role was that of a semi-

The Mechanics of the 1851 Colt Navy Revolver

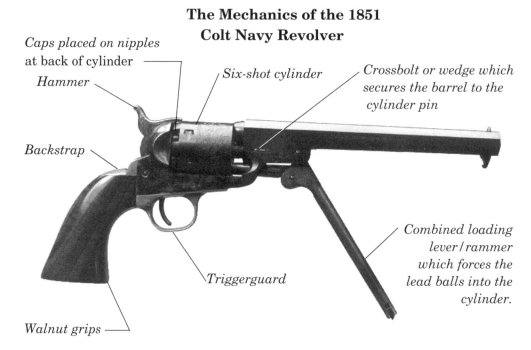

Caps placed on nipples at back of cylinder

Hammer

Six-shot cylinder

Crossbolt or wedge which secures the barrel to the cylinder pin

Backstrap

Combined loading lever / rammer which forces the lead balls into the cylinder.

Triggerguard

Walnut grips

The identification of the parts of the .36 caliber, 1851 Colt Navy, the favorite weapon of James Butler Hickok.

comic sidekick and his attempts to perfect the reverse draw left much to be desired.

In the real West, however, the "reverse" or "Plains" draw was ideally suited for long-barreled pistols, and was much safer than the butt-to-the-rear hip draw. The shooter simply turned his hand so that the palm faced away from his body. As he grasped the butt, his thumb was slipped over the hammer spur and the index finger went through the trigger guard. A sharp pull upwards also spun the barrel forward, and this momentum cocked the pistol as it lined up on its target. The shooter could then fire as it came level, or hold the pistol cocked. The motion of locking the thumb around the hammer spur as the pistol was drawn, meant that it could not be released until the pistol came level. This ensured that one could not shoot one's self (or one's horse) as sometimes happened with the hip draw when cocking the pistol and the thumb slipped from the hammer. The other advantage to wearing pistols butt forward, of course, was that one could also use a cross body draw—ideal when seated!

Anyone who used weapons of any kind kept them in a ready state of repair, for they never knew when they might need to resort to them for survival. Most of the old-time gun-fighters were adept at making minor repairs and adjustments to their fire-arms. The replacement of hammer and trigger springs, triggers, screws and percussion nipples could be accomplished by themselves, so such spares were always readily available. Major problems, such as damaged barrels or cylinders and the occasional snapping of hammer notches (half and full cock), were entrusted to a qualified gunsmith,such as Patrick Hand in Abilene, Kansas.

A facet of the early percussion period that gets little attention is the ammunition used and how it was carried. So far as we know, Wild Bill was never photographed wearing a belt with cartridge loops or a cartridge box attached, so it is likely that he carried his ammunition separately, either factory-made "six packs" of paper or metal foil cartridges, or loose powder in a flask (complete with a measure), precast lead bullets, and boxes of percussion caps. Certainly, he was very careful when using black powder. Many Americans paid extra for the superior English-made powders and Eley Brothers' percussion caps, for both had a reputation for reliability, and the powder in particular was noted for its quality and strength.

Nevertheless, Hickok and his contemporaries shared one common trait, for no matter how good the pow-der and caps were there was always the danger of dampness and misfires, so a second or reserve pistol was a necessity.[5]

Writing in the early 1920s, Charles Gross, who had known Hickok in Abilene, left this interesting observation of Hickok's preoccupation with his pistol "loads." Early one morning, he visited Wild Bill's cabin and learned first hand of his priorities:

> . . . to my surprise as soon as Bill was dressed, all but Coat & Hat—he went carefully to the door[,] looked all around for several m[omen]ts & then Emptied one 6 shooter. He had the one in Each hand, returned to the room[,] cleaned & reloaded it, then went to the door & Empt[i]ed the Other one & reload[ed] it the same way. Bill used powder & Ball—We had pistols then with Metal Ca[r]tridges but Bill would not use them[.] he used powder & Ball, moulded his own bullets & primed Each tube [nipple] using a pin to push the powder in so he was sure of powder contact and before putting on the Cap he looked at the interior of Each Cap[.] now this [was] all strange to me & new too, for I had roomed & slept with Bill all [the] time he was at the [Drover's] Cottage (2 months or more) & he never did it there, so I said, did you get your Guns damp yesterday Bill? He said "no, but I

1. Having half-cocked the hammer to allow the cylinder to spin freely, each chamber is filled with a measure of powder from the flask. (Demonstrated by actor, Randolph Scott.)

2. Working each chamber one at a time, a lead ball is placed on the mouth and is then rammed down by the combined hinged lever-rammer under the barrel.

3. A copper percussion cap containing fulminate of mercury is placed on the nipple at the rear of each chamber.

4. After lowering the hammer and setting the hammer between chambers on one of its safety pins, the revolver is ready for action. (Author's collection.)

ain[']t ready to go yet & I am not taking any chances, when I draw & pull I must be sure . . ."

Perhaps because he was Chief of Police, no one seems to have been concerned when Hickok discharged his pistols within city limits!

Gross also reported that he went out shooting with Hickok one day and was impressed with his marksmanship at twenty feet when shooting at a piece of paper about six inches long with a black spot in the center:

At Hickok's request he called out "Draw!" One moment the pistol was in its holster and the next a startled Gross heard all six shots discharged: "Every shot was in the paper and two in the spot, but all of them within one inch of an up & down line . . . " Left handed, however, Wild Bill had placed all six shots in the paper but none in the black spot. His comment was that he had never "shot" a man with his left hand except when attacked by soldiers at Hays "when I used both hands . . ."[6]

In analyzing Gross's comments it becomes clear that Hickok's reflex reaction to a situation, as hinted at by the writer in the Chicago *Tribune*, was indeed a major factor in his continued survival. This reflex combined with accuracy ensured his success in a gunfight. As he himself once re-marked, he feared no man who was prepared to fight him face-to-face; but he displayed a healthy respect for the backshooter, or coward. Tragically, it was to be at the hands of such an individual that Wild Bill would meet his untimely end.

Notes

1. Ed McGivern, *Fast and Fancy Revolver Shooting* (Chicago, 1975), 302.

2. W. W. Greener, *The Gun and its Development* (London, 1910), 538-539.

3. Joseph G. Rosa, *They Called Him Wild Bill* (Norman, Oklahoma, 1974), 338-349.

4. *Ibid.*, 344.

5. Frank H. Mayer and Charles B. Roth, *The Buffalo Harvest* (Denver, 1958). This book will also appeal to firearms enthusiasts. Many gunfighters paid careful attention to the hammer mainspring and installed a replacement if the original was too strong and hindered a rapid and smooth cocking action.

6. Correspondence between Charles Gross and J. B. Edwards (1922-26). Manuscripts Division, Kansas State Historical Society, Topeka, Kansas.

Chapter Four

ROCK CREEK: THE McCANLES FIGHT

Wild Bill Hickok's fight to the death with the "M'Kandlas Gang" at Rock Creek, Nebraska Territory, on July 12, 1861, marked the beginning of a reputation that six years later would receive nationwide attention. For the incident at Rock Creek, minor by frontier standards, might well have remained obscure but for the publication in *Harper's New Monthly Magazine* for February, 1867, of Colonel George Ward Nichols's article on "Wild Bill." The pair met at Springfield, Missouri, in the late summer of 1865 when Nichols, accompanied General Thomas Church Haskell Smith, the Inspector General of the District of South-West Missouri, who was on an inspection tour. Springfield was then winding down as the district headquarters and was a hive of activity.

Nichols recalled that "Wild Bill" and several army officers gave him an account of his wartime adventures. Among them was a "Captain Honesty," a *nom de plume* Nichols invented for Captain Richard Bentley Owen, Hickok's quartermaster during the late conflict.

These stories formed the basis for the article. But by far the most amazing of them was the so-called "M'Kandlas Massacre." Here is how Nichols described it:

> I was especially Desirous to hear him relate the history of a sanguinary fight which he had with a party of ruffians in the early part of the war, when, single-handed, he fought and killed ten men. I had heard the story as it came from an officer of the regular army who, an hour after the affair, saw Bill and the ten dead men—some killed with bullets, others hacked and slashed to death with a knife.
>
> As I write out the details of this ter-

This woodcut of Colonel George Ward Nicholas, based upon a photograph, was published in **Harper's Weekly** *on September 26, 1885, in an obituary to him following his death from tuberculosis at Cincinnati on the 15th of that month.*

rible tale from notes which I took as the words fell from the scout's lips, I am conscious of its extreme improbability; but while I listened to him I remembered the story in the Bible, where we are told that Samson "with the jawbone of an ass slew a thousand men," and as I looked upon this magnificent example of human strength and daring, he appeared to me to realize the powers of a Samson and Hercules combined, and I should not have been inclined to place any limit upon his achievements. Besides this, one who has lived for four years in the presence of such grand heroism and deeds of prowess as was seen during the war in what might be called a "receptive" mood. Be the story true or not, in part, or in whole,

I believed then every word Wild Bill uttered, and I believe it today.

"I don't like to talk about that M'Kandlas affair," said Bill, in answer to my question. "It gives me a queer shiver whenever I think of it, and sometimes I dream about it, and wake up in a cold sweat.

"You see this M'Kandlas was the Captain of a gang of desperadoes, horse-thieves, murderers, regular cut-throats, who were the terror of every body on the border, and who kept us in the mountains in hot water whenever they were around. I knew them all in the mountains, where they pretended to be trapping, but they were hiding from the hangman. M'Kandlas was the biggest scoundrel and bully of them all, and was allers a-braggin of what he could do. One day I beat him shootin at a mark, and then threw him at the back-holt. And I didn't drop him as soft as you would a baby, you may be sure. Well, he got savage mad about it, and swore he would have his revenge on me some time.

"This was just before the war broke out, and we were already takin sides in the mountains either for the South or the Union. M'Kandlas and his gang were border-ruffians in the Kansas row, and of course they went with the rebs. Bime-by he clar'd out, and I shouldn't have thought of the feller agin ef he hadn't crossed my path. It 'pears he didn't forget me.

"It was in '61, when I guided a detachment of cavalry who were comin in from Camp Floyd. We had nearly reached the Kansas line, and were in South Nebraska, when one afternoon I went out of camp to go to the cabin of an old friend of mine, a Mrs. Waltman. I took only one of my revolvers with me, for although the war had broke out I didn't think it necessary to carry both my pistols, and, in all or'nary scrimmages, one is better than a dozen ef you shoot straight. I saw some wild turkeys on the road as I was goin down, and popped one of 'em over, thinkin he'd be just the thing for supper.

"Well, I rode up to Mrs. Waltman's, jumped off my horse, and went into the cabin, which is like most of the cabins on the prarer, with only one room, and that had two doors, one opening in front and t'other on a yard, like.

"'How are you, Mrs. Waltman?' I said, feeling as jolly as you please.

"The minute she saw me she turned as white as a sheet and screamed: 'Is that you, Bill? Oh, my God! They will kill you! Run! Run! They will kill you!'

"'Who's a-goin to kill me?' said I. 'There's two can play at that game.'

"'It's M'Kandlas and his gang. There's ten of them, and you've no chance. they've jes gone down the road to the corn-rack. They came up here only five minutes ago. M'Kandlas was draggin poor Parson Shipley on the ground with a lariat round his neck. The preacher was most dead with choking and the horses stamping on him. M'Kandlas knows yer bringin in that party of Yankee cavalry, and he swears he'll cut yer heart out. Run, Bill, run—But it's too late; they're comin up the lane.'

"While she was a-talkin I remembered I had but one revolver, and a load gone out of that. On the table there was a horn of powder and some little bars of lead. I poured some powder into the empty chamber and rammed the lead after it by hammering the barrel on the table, and had just capped the pistol when I heard M'Kandlas shout: "'There's that d—

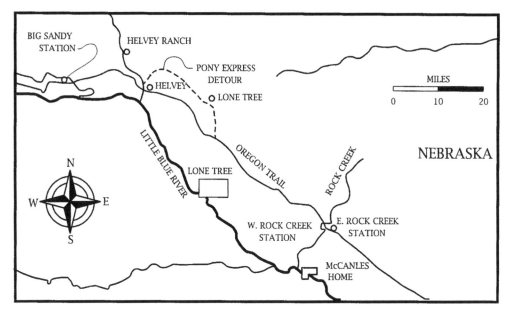

The location of the Rock Creek Station in Nebraska.

—d Yank Wild Bill's horse; he's here, and we'll skin him alive!'

"If I had thought of runnin before it war too late now, and the house was my best holt—a sort of fortress, like. I never thought I should leave that room alive."

The scout stopped his story, rose from his seat, and strode back and forward in a state of great excitement.

"I tell you what it is, Kernel," he resumed, after a while, "I don't mind a scrimmage with those fellers round here. Shoot one or two of them and the rest run away. But all of M'Kandlas's gang were reckless, blood-thirsty devils, who would fight as long as they had strength to pull a trigger. I have been in tight places, but that's one of the few times I said

my prayers.

"'Surround the house and give him no quarter!' yelled M'Kandlas. When I heard that I felt as quiet and cool as if I was a-goin to church. I looked round the room and saw a Hawkins [Hawken] rifle hangin over the bed.

"'Is that loaded?' said I to Mrs. Waltman.

"'Yes,' the poor thing whispered. She was so frightened she couldn't speak out loud.

"'Are you sure?' said I, as I jumped to the bed and caught it from its hooks. Although my eye did not leave the door, yet I could see she nodded 'Yes' again. I put the revolver on the bed, and just then M'Kandlas poked his head inside the doorway, but jumped back when he saw me with the rifle in my hand. "'Come in here,

William Monroe's sketch of the Rock Creek Station as he recalled it about fifty years later. (Courtesy the Nebraska State Historical Society.)

you cowardly dog!' I shouted. 'Come in here, and fight me!'" M'Kandlas was no coward, if he was a bully. He jumped inside the room with his gun leveled to shoot; but he was not quick enough. My rifle-ball went through his heart. He fell back outside the house, where he was found afterward holding tight to his rifle, which had fallen over his head.

"His disappearance was followed by a yell from his gang and then there was a dead silence. I put down the rifle and took the revolver, and I said to myself: 'Only six shots and nine men to kill. Save your powder, Bill, for the death-hug's a-comin'!' I don't know why it was, Kernel," continued Bill, looking at me inquiringly, "but at that moment things seemed clear and sharp. I could think strong.

"There was a few seconds of that awful stillness, then the ruffians came rushing at both doors. How wild they looked with their red, drunken faces and inflamed eyes, shouting and cussing! But I never aimed more deliberately in my life.

"One—two—three—four; and four men fell dead.

"That didn't stop the rest. Two of them fired their bird-guns at me. And then I felt a sting run all over me. The room was full of smoke. Two got in close to me, their eyes glaring out of the clouds. One I knocked down with my fist. 'You are out of the way for a while,' I thought. The second I shot dead. The other three clutched me and crowded me onto the bed. I fought hard. I broke with my hand one man's arm. He had his fingers round my throat. Before I could get to my feet I was struck across the breast with the stock of a rifle, and I felt the blood rushing out of my nose

The Rock Creek Station photographed sometime after the McCanles affair. The original plate is a tintype which has been reversed here to correct its "mirror" image and make the scene appear as it should. The horseman has not been identified. (Courtesy the California State Library.)

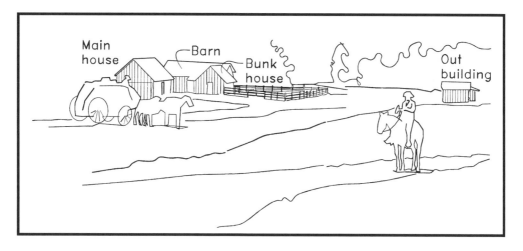

The structures at the Rock Creek station shown in the photograph above are labeled in this drawing to clarify the site of the Hickok-McCanles Fight.

and mouth. Then I got ugly, and I remember that I got hold of a knife, and then it was all cloudy like, and I was wild, and I struck savage blows, following the devils up from one side to the other of the room and into the corners, striking and slashing until I knew that every one was dead.

"All of a sudden it seemed as if my heart was on fire. I was bleeding ev-

This 1999 view of Rock Creek was made in approximately the same position as the original photograph depicting a horseman and a stagecoach. The buildings are close copies of the originals. (Courtesy Vincent Bergdale.)

An overview of the Rock Creek Station looking toward the east. (Courtesy Vincent Bergdale.)

erywhere. I rushed out to the well and drank from the bucket, and then tumbled down in a faint."

Breathless with the intense interest with which I had followed this strange story, all the more thrilling and weird when its hero, seeming to live over again the bloody events of that day, gave way to its terrible spirit with wild, savage gestures. I saw then—what my scrutiny of the morning had failed to discover—the tiger which lay concealed beneath that gentle exterior.

David C. McCanles, from a family portrait circa 1859. (Courtesy the Nebraska State Historical Society.)

Monroe, son of David McCanles, survived the Rock Creek fight. (Courtesy the Nebraska State Historical Society.)

"You must have been hurt almost to death," I said.

"'There were eleven buck-shot in me. I carry some of them now. I was cut in thirteen places. All of them bad enough to have let out the life of a man. But that blessed old Dr. Mills pulled me safe through it, after a bed siege of many a long week."

Nichols (or his editor) could not count—according to Wild Bill he used only five of his six shots! But the most glaring error in Nichols's alleged quote from Wild Bill is his description of Hickok loading his pistol by "hammering the barrel on the table." This would have been a waste of time and effort and only succeed in blocking the muzzle. What he really meant was that Hickok set the pistol at half-cock (so that the cylinder could spin freely), poured powder into the chamber, placed a lead ball (or a small "lead bar") in the mouth of the chamber, and rammed it in with the hinged rammer and lever attached beneath the barrel. He then placed a cap on the nipple at the rear of the cylinder, and the pistol was ready for action.

*The "McCanles Massacre" as depicted in **Harper's New Monthly Magazine** for Febrary 1867. (Author's Collection.)*

Nichols' yarn inspired many imitators and variations of the affair were common. One of the more bizarre versions came from Buffalo Bill Cody. In an interview published in the Rochester, New York, *Democrat & Chronicle* on September 18, 1876, he stated that:

Hickok killed the McCandless gang, who murdered my father in the early Kansas troubles, in '56. Bill was a pony express rider on the old Denver and Atchison trail, or what was called the Salt lake trail and the California trail. He was one day approaching a station on Rock Creek when he heard a woman scream. Over the door-sill of the stable he saw a man's dead body and the screams were coming from the house. He rushed in and rescued the woman from McCanles and six of his gang. They rushed after him and he dropped four of them, one after another, as they came through the door.

Three then made for him but with his knife he finished two of them and the other ran. He thus cleaned out a gang which was the terror of the country, and did it in saving a woman . . . "

Over the years Cody was to provide other versions, and upped the tally to ten; but why he should claim that McCanles murdered his father (who died several years after being stabbed at an antislavery rally), only he would know.

Available Documentation

An examination of available documents and other materials relative to the shooting at Rock Creek has failed to establish whether it was Hickok or Horace Wellman, the station keeper, who shot McCanles. But evidence has been unearthed which casts doubt on Hickok's reason for being at the station (and his actual date of arrival), and recent research into McCanles's earlier activities does little to enhance his already dubious reputation.

Curiously, by 1867 when Nichols's account was published, the story was already well known in parts of the West, especially Kansas, where the *Harper's* version was greeted with some skepticism. The Atchison *Daily Champion* of February 5, 1867, declared that there were only four men involved and not fourteen [*sic*—ten]

as stated by Nichols, and that Hickok shot the leader with his rifle, two others with his revolver and wounded the fourth man who fled and disappeared. Perhaps unwittingly, the editor did make one correct statement when he declared that the fight was not between "the McKandlas gang" and Hickok, but between the gang and the owners of the stage line.

David C. McCanles, the main character in the tragedy, was born in Iredell County, North Carolina, in 1828, but soon afterward his family moved to Watauga County where he later served as county sheriff. A great socializer, McCanless was reported to be six feet tall and heavily built. He was also said to be a hard character. Although a married man with children, he flouted the conventions of the day and had a mistress, Sarah Shull, the daughter of a local mill owner.

Only in recent years has it been confirmed (but rumored in the Rock Creek area after his death) that she bore him a child which died in its infancy. By 1859, pressures on his marriage, and his community status, prompted him to abandon his family and flee West with Sarah, together with funds owed to the county. By the time he reached Rock Creek, at that time a small relay station on the Oregon Trail, disillusioned gold-seekers from the Pike's Peak rush convinced

*Wild Bill's fight with the McCanles gang as depicted in Buel's **Heroes of the Plains**. (Author's collection.)*

him that there would be no point in going on, so he negotiated with the current owner and bought the station. Once he and Sarah had settled in, however, he then sent for his family. This move on Dave's part is interesting. Having fled in disgrace, did his conscience bother him when he realized that his family members were now social outcasts? Yet by sending for them, he ran the risk of discovery.

Or had he planned before his departure to send for them knowing that they would not divulge his whereabouts to the authorities? Whatever the reason, no one has yet learned what his wife really thought

of Sarah (listed in Census returns as a "domestic"), or indeed of her presence at the station.

Once established, however, McCanles set about modifying his property, and within a year he had improved the water supply, set up a toll bridge, and later he was able to build another ranch to the east of the original buildings. In April, 1861, Russell, Majors and Waddell's Central Overland California and Pike's Peak Express Company, who had originally rented the Eastside ranch for use as a relay station on their newly established Pony Express route, told McCanles that they now wished to buy it. A one-third down

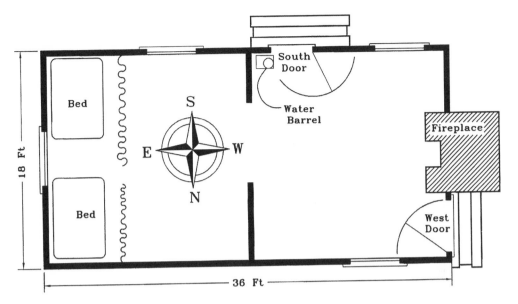

*This diagram is based upon the one that appeared in Charles Dawson's **Pioneer Tales of the Oregon Trail** published in 1912. Designed as a two-room dwelling, it is was about 36 ft. x 18 ft. It was divided by a partition that had a 6 ft. opening that served as an access to both rooms. The beds were behind the curtains.*

payment was made with an agreement to pay the remainder over three months.

In March of 1861, the company's superintendent, Horace Wellman, and his common-law-wife, Jane, arrived at the station. Close on their heels, according to most historians, came James Butler Hickok, still suffering from the effects of a fight with a bear, and sent to the place by the company to recuperate. We now know that there was no bear fight, and the late Ethel Hickok produced a letter from Jones and Cartwright (whose freighting business rivalled that of Russell Majors and Waddell's) which proved that until late April 1861, James was in their employ.

His cousin Guy Butler also stated that James Hickok had worked for them since 1858. This disclosure not only refutes the long-held belief that Hickok was employed by Russell, Majors and Waddell prior to his appearance at Rock Creek, but it also prompts questions. Both Russell, Majors and Waddell and Jones and Cartwright went bankrupt in 1861. Therefore, if Hickok was employed by RM&W in 1861, it must have been in a temporary capacity, unless he just appeared at the station in-between career moves and was hired by Wellman. We may never know the answer to that; but his continued

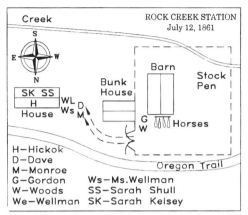

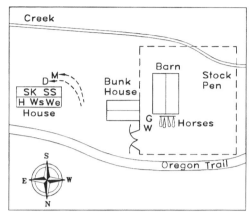

1. *July 12, 1861, 4:00 pm, July 12, 1861: Dave McCanles and son, Monroe, and employees James Woods and James Gordon arrive at Rock Creek. Woods and Gordon stay at the barn; Dave and Monroe meet the Wellmans at the west door. Dave demands the station be returned due to nonpayment by Russell, Majors & Waddell. Horace says that he has no such authority. Jane abuses Dave for being harsh to her father. Horace retreats into the house.*

2. *4:10 pm: As Jane continues her heated exchange with Dave McCanles, Hickok appears from within the house. Hickok joins in the argument and berates Dave for his attack on the Wellmans. Hickok goes back into the house; Dave and Monroe walk around the house to the south door and resume their arguments with Mrs. Wellman from the steps outside.*

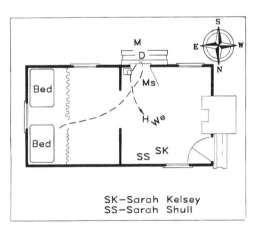

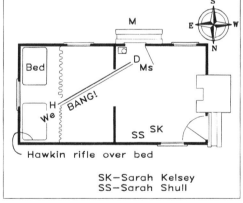

3. *4:15 pm: From the door, Dave sees Hickok and Wellman in earnest conversation. Dave asks for a drink of water. Hickok gives it to him, and walks toward the curtained area with Wellman. Jane continues her heated argument with Dave. Dave calls to Hickok to come back.*

4. *4:20 pm: Hickok and Wellman obtain a rifle and a pistol from behind the curtain. Either Hickok or Wellman shoots Dave from behind the curtain with the rifle. Dave falls backward into the yard, mortally wounded. Monroe rushes to his father's side and Dave dies.*

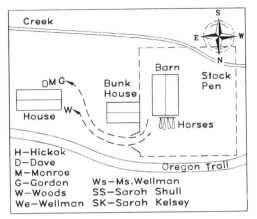

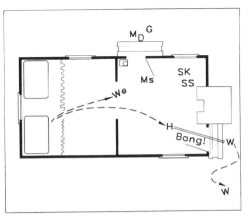

5. *4:20 pm: Down at the barn, Woods and Gordon hear the shot and run toward the house. Woods goes to the west door and Gordon runs to the south door to find Monroe crouching over Dave's lifeless body.*

6. *4:22 pm: James Woods steps into the doorway; either Hickok or Wellman shoots him and Woods staggers backward, severely wounded by the gunshot. Gordon is at the south door when he hears the gunshot.*

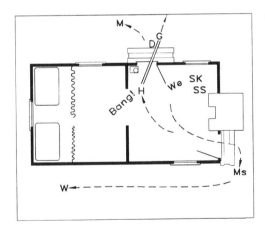

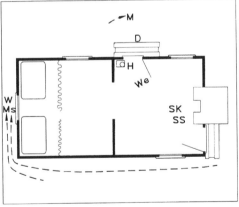

7. *4:22 pm: Curious about the shot that he heard, Gordon looks in through the south door. Hickok walks to the south door and shoots through the door and wounds Gordon. Gordon stumbles toward the brush to escape. Meanwhile Woods staggers to the side of the house.*

8. *4:23 pm: Ms. Wellman pursues the wounded Woods with a grubbing hoe. When she overtakes him, she goes beserk and kills him with the grubbing hoe. Only twelve-year old Monroe is left unharmed at this time.*

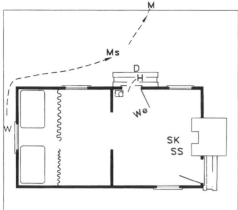

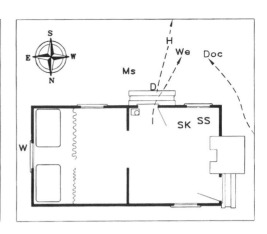

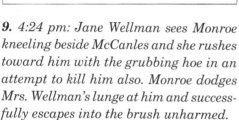

9. *4:24 pm: Jane Wellman sees Monroe kneeling beside McCanles and she rushes toward him with the grubbing hoe in an attempt to kill him also. Monroe dodges Mrs. Wellman's lunge at him and successfully escapes into the brush unharmed.*

10. *4:30 pm: Hickok, Doc Brink, and Wellman follow Gordon's dog that leads them to Gordon lying in the brush. Gordon is killed with a shotgun and buried on the spot. Monroe later reaches his home and tells his terrible story.*

presence at the station when it became known that RM&W were in financial difficulties does suggest that he may have been employed by Wellman rather than RM&W. But conjecture is not fact, and perhaps with time more information concerning Hickok's true status at Rock Creek may come to light.[1]

By June 1861, the financial state of Russell Majors and Waddell's Central Overland California and Pike's Peak Express Company was common knowledge. Disgruntled employees were dubbing the company the "Cleaned out and Poor Pay Outfit." Later in the month, McCanles, concerned over the company's payment

arrears, persuaded Horace Wellman to go to Brownville to request payment or an explanation from Benjamin Ficklin, the company's line superintendent. It was arranged that McCanles's twelve-year-old son, William Monroe, should accompany Wellman to obtain supplies and to identify some of his father's stock and harness still in the possession of the Rocky Mountain Dispatch Company who had rented the station prior to RM&W and left owing him money. They left on July 1.

During Wellman's absence, McCanles anticipated the outcome of his visit to Brownville, and on several occasions appeared at the sta-

A life-size reconstruction of the moment McCanles was shot--as some Nebraskans believe it happened, but McCanles may have been shot by Wellman and not Hickok. (Courtesy the Nebraska State Historical Society.)

tion and requested that it be turned over to him. But Jane Wellman, who detested McCanles, refused (he had recently beaten up her father whom he had charged with theft). Hickok took no part in any of these discussions. Then, late in the afternoon of July 11, Wellman and the boy returned to report that Ficklin could not promise any money or suggest a date of payment.

On the afternoon of the 12th McCanles, accompanied by his son and two employees, James Woods and James Gordon, arrived at the station. Leaving both men at the barn with the horses, he and Monroe walked over to the house. He was met at the west door by the Wellmans. During the verbal exchange over the ownership of the station, Horace retreated into the house, while Jane rebuked McCanles for his treatment of her father. At this point Hickok appeared, and after exchanging a few words, Dave asked him for a drink of water. Hickok stepped inside the house to get it. Inside the house, some have claimed, Hickok was confronted by a very scared Wellman. McCanles, meanwhile, had left the west door and moved to the south door. Here conjecture and opinion vie with fact: the inside of the house was divided by a curtain, behind which, it is alleged, Wellman had a rifled musket (owned or loaned by McCanles) and Hickok had a pair of pistols.

The scenario now revolves around whether or not McCanles, Woods and Gordon were armed. Some sources claim they all were, and others that they were not. If they were, did McCanles threaten Hickok and Wellman, or did one of them shoot him without provocation? Since no written statement by Hickok or Wellman has come to light, or for that matter by any of the other witnesses called to give evidence, only McCanles, Hickok, and Wellman know what happened inside the room. When a shot was fired, McCanles fell backwards to the ground, and died soon afterwards. Woods and Gordon ran from the barn. Hickok is alleged to have shot and wounded Woods who was then attacked by Mrs. Wellman. Gordon turned to run and was also wounded by Hickok who had been joined by James W. ("Doc") Brink a pony express rider.

William Monroe rushed to his father's side, but was driven away by Jane Wellman. He turned and fled into the brush dodging several shots fired at him, and ran home to report what had happened. Jane Wellman is then alleged to have chased and killed the wounded Woods with a hoe. Hickok and others pursued Gordon into the brush, where his pet dog disclosed his whereabouts. Someone then killed him with a shotgun. He was buried where he fell.

Hickok is said to have confronted Joe Baker, one of McCanles's employees, and threatened him, but he was "spared" when Sarah Kelsey, his stepdaughter (who had been in the station during the shooting), begged for his life. Hickok lowered the hammer of his pistol and instead hit him over the head with the barrel remarking: "Well, you've got to take that anyway." Like many other claims made about the events at Rock Creek, that story lacks verification, as do the yarns concerning McCanles's alleged Confederate sympathies and sadism toward those who upset him.

The McCanles faction have always maintained that Dave and his two companions, Woods and Gordon, were unarmed. Yet it was his habit to go armed with two revolvers and a short double-barreled shotgun which he usually carried on his saddle horn. The truth or otherwise of that has yet to be established. But it does seem odd that for a man who normally went armed, McCanles, determined to retrieve by force if necessary what he still regarded as his own property, should be unarmed.

A well entrenched facet of the Rock Creek fight is the claim that

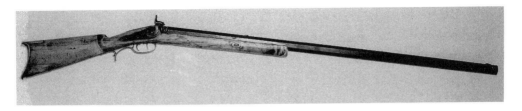

The half-stocked .56 caliber rifle believed made by Postley, Nerlson & Co. (located in Pennsylvania), is said to have been brought to Rock Creek by McCanles who left it at the station. The rifle was donated to the Society by George W. Hanson who received it from the McCanles family. (Courtesy the Nabraska State Historical Society.)

McCanles dubbed Hickok "Duck Bill" on account of the shape of his nose, or his "protruding lips." This is ludicrous, Hickok's nose was Roman or aquiline in shape, which is revealed by an examination of unretouched photographs. I suspect that this yarn originated over the misspelling of "Dutch Bill" to "Duch" on some of the documents relative to the subsequent hearing.

But why Hickok was called "Dutch Bill" at Rock Creek is a valid question that awaits an answer.

The few mentions of Hickok discovered in the Kansas territorial newspapers reveal that as early as 1857 he was known to his neighbors at Monticello as "Bill" or "William." As for "Dutch Bill," perhaps the answer had something to do with his personal appearance and coloring.

When Hickok, Brink, and Wellman were arrested on July 15, 1861 by E. B. Hendee, Sheriff of Gage County, on a warrant issued on July 13 following a Complaint made by the McCanles family, they were taken by wagon to Beatrice, and remanded in custody pending an appearance before Justice of the Peace T. M. Coulter. The hearing took place between July 15, 16 and 18. Among those who attended was twelve-year old Hugh J. Dobbs who had originally arrived in Gage County, Nebraska, in 1859 aged nine. His recollections and description of Hickok, whom he referred to as "Wild Bill" was doubtless influenced by the name he was known by in later years:

I remember that "Wild Bill" sat opposite to where I stood, and he was dressed in a gray suit; he was of light complexion, sandy bearded and with sandy hair; his eyes were quick and intense. There were times when he rose and paced the floor, and his tall, slim figure, well proportioned and quick in movement, made a deep impression on me. . . .

"Wild Bill" appeared nervous in the beginning of his trial, but this passed away as the trial progressed and he became calm and deliberate. I never heard in the whispers that went around the court room or in the yard outside, that "Wild Bill" had been attacked by a bear and had been almost disemboweled from this encounter, and that but a short time before he had been sent to Rock Creek Station to recuperate. He was to all appearances a strong, healthy man, in the prime of life, and had no appearance of an invalid or of one recovering from physical disability. If such had been the case, I believe there would have been talk of it among the onlookers and loiterers who came for miles around on the prairie—keen for talk of the happenings of prairie life; and as a prairie boy, almost twelve years of age, I would have remembered any bear story.[2]

Jane Wellman was called to testify on behalf of the Territory, and although Munroe [sic] McCanles was subpoenaed to attend, he was not called upon to give evidence. None of the witnesses' testimony was recorded; but by the time Hickok, Wellman, and Brink had pleaded that their actions were taken in defense of company property, Justice Coulter had decided that the charge of "murder was not sustained" and discharged them.

"Doc" Brink's role in the affair has never been explained, and efforts to trace him following the shooting have failed. In the case of the Wellmans, if Jane was indeed the daughter of Joseph Holmes, a search of local records has so far failed to trace her or Wellman. She and Horace simply disappeared. But Sarah Shull has been traced and her brief comments on the affair are interesting. When interviewed by Frank J. Wilstach in 1925 she claimed she was some miles away when the shooting took place, and that McCanles was a Confederate sympathizer. Shortly before her death in 1932, however, she admitted that both she and Sarah Kelsey were in the house. But both women were bundled into the root cellar when McCanles and the Wellmans started to argue. They heard the shot that killed McCanles, but were unable to state who fired it. Sarah never offered an opinion concerning Hickok's role in the shooting, although her personal recollection of him is revealing:

> Hickok had steel-blue eyes that were beautiful and gentle but could change in a second and look dangerous. You had better watch his eyes; he wasn't one to run from a fight. I came close to having an affair with Hickok.[3]

Once he was released, Hickok left the area and went to Leavenworth where he signed on as a teamster with the Union Army. Promoted to wagonmaster, he was later transferred to the Provost Marshal's department as a detective and, finally, as a scout, courier, and spy. Back at Rock Creek, the Wellmans and Brink also moved on, but Sarah Shull remained until late August when David McCanles's brother, James, paid her money still owed her by his late brother. She then disappeared until discovered by Wilstach. Later, she was befriended by Jessie Williams who eventually persuaded her to let her tell her story.[4]

The Rock Creek affair remains an enigma. Such is the evidence that one can make a case for or against Hickok, because both he and Wellman were inside the house when the fatal shot that killed McCanles was fired. Wellman, perhaps, had more reason than Hickok to fear or hate McCanles, whereas Hickok may well have believed that his actions were in defense of company property. But minor or not, that incident did more for Hickok's legend than anything else.

Notes

1. The material on the "McCanles Massacre" is vast. However, the following publications will provide a general overview: George W. Hansen, "The True Story of Wild Bill's McCanles Affray in Jefferson County, Nebraska, July 12, 1861." *Nebraska History Magazine* (April-June 1927); William E. Connelley, "Wild Bill—James Butler Hickok: David C. McCanles at Rock Creek," Kansas State Historical Society *Collections* 17 (1926-28); Mark Dugan, *Tales Never Told Around the Campfire* (Athens, Ohio, 1990). See also *They Called Him Wild Bill, 34-52.*

2. Manuscripts Division, Nebraska State Historical Society, Lincoln, Nebraska.

3. Dugan, *Tales Never Told Around the Campfire, loc. cit.,* 29-78.

4. *Ibid.*

Chapter Five

THE HICKOK-TUTT DUEL

The era of the gunfighter spanned the period 1851 until approximately 1900 (with a few "post era" characters who operated until World War I). Many men contributed to the gunfighter myth, and some of them became legendary. Yet few of them fit the mold of what we believe a gunfighter is and should be. Hollywood Westerns have for so long conditioned us to accept gunfighters as knight errants and gunfights fought between equals in a sportsmanlike fashion (a duel to the death in which both participants faced each other on an even footing), that it is difficult to accept anything else.

In reality, few gunfights were fought amongst equals, or were conducted as stand-up, scheduled duels where a test of nerve and marksmanship was paramount. Instead, one or both of the protagonists might be drunk, or inexperienced, hesitant and afraid, which could cost him his life. And some men were not given the chance to defend themselves because they were shot in the back. Few if any saw gunfighting as a "sport," rather it was a means of disposing of an opponent—preferably with a minimum of personal risk.

Speed on the draw—a facet of gunfighting that obsesses some modern re-enactors—played little part in old-time gunfights. Hickok's comment to Nichols in his *Harper's* article is as true today as it was in 1865: "Whenever you get into a row be sure and not shoot too quick. Take time. I've known many a feller to slip up for shootin' in a hurry." And to Charles Gross in 1871, Hickok declared: "Charlie, I hope you never have to shoot any man, but if you do, [try and] shoot him in the Guts near

Wild Bill dressed and armed as he appeared at Springfield in 1864-65. He wears his coat buttoned right to left (as he did in the Harper's woodcut), and his military-buckled belt and open-topped holsters are typical of the time (many preferred flap holsters which gave better protection to their weapons against dust, dirt, and dampness). Hickok could use either a cross draw or a reverse draw when wearing pistols waist high. (Courtesy James Joplin and Bob McCubbin, who now owns the photograph.)

the Navel, you may not make a fatal shot, but he will get a shock that will paralyze his brain and arm so much that the fight is all over."[1]

When Wild Bill shot Davis K. Tutt on Public Square, Springfield, Missouri, on the evening of July 21, 1865, following a dispute over a game of cards the previous evening, it was as close to our Hollywood inspired notion of a duel-type gunfight as any on record. Yet, it remained the subject of controversy (and many lies) for more than a century. Supporters of both men have voiced opinion or written sometimes contradictory accounts which, because of a lack of evidence, have only clouded the issue still further.

Much of the alleged enmity between both men was created by the press and old-timers who still harbored Union or Confederate sympathies. Tutt was a native of Yellville, Arkansas, where he was born in 1839. According to Confederate military records at the National Archives, he was mustered into the Confederate Army at age 22 on June 12, 1862, and served for a year as a private in Company A of the 27th Arkansas Infantry. By February 1863 he had been detailed to the Quartermaster Department as a brigade wagonmaster. From April 30 he was listed in that capacity as on "detached service."

He then disappeared from Confederate records. By 1864, however, Tutt was settled in Springfield where he gained a reputation as a gambler and friend of Wild Bill's. It now seems that Dave did in fact desert the Confederacy for the Union. For two years after his death, the Springfield *Tri-Weekly Patriot* of January 24, 1867, included the name of "D.K. Tutt" among a long list of individuals named on vouchers in possession of R. B. Owen, late Chief Quartermaster District of South-West Missouri.

Colonel George Ward Nichols' article in *Harper's New Monthly Magazine* was the first to publicize the Hickok-Tutt duel nationwide. Although his account of the fight was based upon firsthand information,[2] the injection of some fiction invalidates much of it. But it is important that we cite his version. Nichols learned of the duel from "Captain Honesty [R. B. Owen] who was as unprejudiced, if it is possible to find an unbiased mind in a town of 3000 people after a fight has taken place." Nichols then quoted the gallant captain verbatim in a crude dialect (as he did with Hickok) that presumably was added for "color":

"They say Bill's wild. Now he isn't any sich thing. I've known him going on ter ten year, and he's as civil a disposed person as you'll find hee-arbouts. But he won't be put upon."

"I'll tell yer how it happened. But come inter the office; thar's a good many round hy'ar as sides with Tutt—the man that's shot. But I tell yer 'twas a fa[i]r fight. Take some whisky? No! Well, I will, if yer'l excuse me."

"You see," continued the Captain, setting the empty glass on the table in an emphatic way, "Bill was up in his room a-playin seven up, or four-hand, or some of them pesky games.

Richard Bentley Owen, Hickok's quartermaster at various times during the War, who was immortalized by Nichols as "Captain Honesty." (Courtesy James Joplin.)

Bill refused ter play with Tutt, who was a professional gambler. Yer see, Bill was a scout on our side durin the war, and Tutt was a reb scout. Bill had killed Dave Tutt's mate, and, atween one thing and another, there war an onusual hard feelin atwixt 'em."

"Ever sin Dave come back he had tried to pick a row with Bill; so Bill wouldn't play cards with him any more. But Dave stood over the man who was gambling with Bill and lent the feller money. Bill won bout two hundred dollars, which made Tutt spiteful mad. Bime-by, he says to Bill:

"'Bill, you've got plenty of money— pay me that forty dollars yer owe me in that horse trade.'

"And Bill paid him. Then he said:

"Yer owe me thirty-five dollars more; yer lost it playing with me t'other night."

"Dave's style was right provoking; but Bill answered him perfectly gentlemanly: 'I think yer wrong Dave. It's only twenty-five dollars. I have a memorandum of it in my pocket down stairs. Ef it's thirty-five dollars I'll give it yer.'"

"Now Bill's watch was lying on the table. Dave took up the watch, put it in his pocket, and said: 'I'll keep this yere watch till yer pay me that thirty-five dollars.'"

"This made Bill shooting mad; fur don't yer see, Colonel, it was a-doubting his honor like, so he got up and looked Dave in the eyes, and said to him: 'I don't want ter make a row in this house. It's a decent house, and I don't want ter injure the keeper. You'd better put that watch back on the table."

"But Dave grinned at Bill mighty ugly, and walked off with the watch, and kept it several days. All this time Dave's friends wre spurring Bill on ter fight; there was no end ter the talk. They blackguarded him in an underhand sort of a way, and tried ter get up a scrimmage, and then they thought they could lay him out. Yer see Bill has enemies all about. He's settled the accounts of a heap of men who lived round here. This is about the only place in Missouri whar a reb can come back and live, and ter tell yer the truth, Colonel—" and the Captain, with an involuntary movement, hitched up his revolver-belt, as he said, with expressive significance, "they don't stay long round here!"

"Well, as I was saying, these rebs don't like ter see a man walking round town who they knew in the reb army as one of their men, who they now know was on our side, all the time he was sending us information, sometimes from Pap Price's own head-quarters. But they couldn't provoke Bill inter a row, for he's afeard of hisself when he gits *awful* mad; and he allers left his shootin irons in his room when he went out. One day these cusses drew their pistols on him and dared him to fight, and then they told him that Tutt was a-goin ter pack that watch across the squar next day at noon.

"I heard of this, for every body was talking about it on the street, and so I went after Bill, and found him in his room cleaning and greasing and loading his revolvers."

"'Now, Bill,' says I, 'you're goin ter git inter a fight.'"

"'Don't you bother yerself, Captain,' says he. 'It's not the first time I have been in a fight; and these d——d hounds have put on me long enough. You don't want me ter give up my honor, do yer?'"

"'No, Bill,' says I, 'yer must keep yer honor.'"

"Next day, about noon, Bill went down on the squar. He had said that Dave Tutt shouldn't pack that watch across the squar unless dead men could walk."

"When Bill got onter the squar he found a crowd stanin in the corner of the street by which he entered the squar, which is from the south, yer know. In this crowd he saw a lot of Tutt's friends; some were cousins of his'n, just back from the reb army; and they jeered him, and boasted that Dave was a-goin to pack that watch across the squar as he promised."

"Then Bill saw Tutt stanin near the court-house, which yer remember is on the west side, so that the crowd war behind Bill."

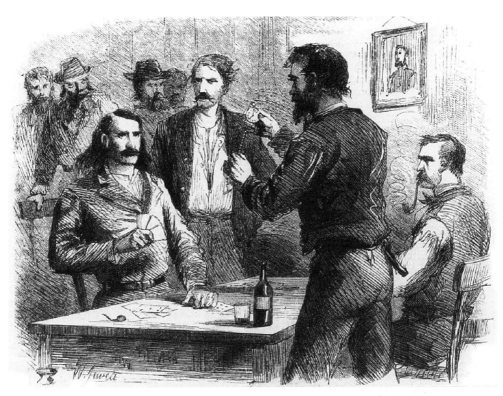

*Dave Tutt picks up Hickok's watch, as depicted in **Harper's New Monthly Magazine.** (Author's collection.)*

"Just then Tutt, who war alone, started from the court-house and walked out into the squar, and Bill moved away from the crowd toward the west side of the squar. Bout fifteen paces brought them opposite to each other, and bout fifty yards apart. Tutt then showed his pistol. Bill had kept a sharp eye on him, and before Tutt could pint it Bill has his'n out."

"At that moment you could have heard a pin drop in that squar. Both Tutt and Bill fired, but one discharge followed the other so quick that it's hard to say which went off first. Tutt was a famous shot, but he missed this time; the ball from his pistol went over Bill's head. The instant Bill fired, without waitin ter see ef he had hit Tutt, he wheeled on his heels and pointed his pistol at Tutt's friends, who had already drawn their weepons."

"'Aren't yer satisfied, gentlemen?' cried Bill, as cool as an alligator. 'Put up your shootin-irons, or there'll be more dead men here.' And they put 'em up, and said it war a far fight."

"What became of Tutt?" I asked of the Captain, who had stopped at this point of his story, and was very deliberately engaged in refilling his empty glass."

"Oh! Dave? He was as plucky a feller as ever drew trigger; but Lord bless yer! It was no use. Bill never shoots twice at the same man, and his ball went through Dave's heart. He stood stock-still for a second or two, then raised his arm as if ter fire again, then he swayed a little, staggered three or four steps, and then fell dead."

"Bill and his friends wanted ter have the thing done regular, so we went up ter the Justice, and Bill delivered himself up. A jury was drawn, Bill was tried and cleared the next day. It was proved that it was a case of self-defense. Don't yer see, Colonel"

I answered that I was afraid that I did not see that point very clearly.

"Well, well!" he replied, with an air of compassion, "you haven't drunk any whisky, that's what's the matter with yer." And then, putting his hand on my shoulder with a half-mysterious half-conscious look in his face, he muttered, in a whisper: "'The *fact is, thar was an undercurrent of a woman in that fight.'*"

Many of the writers who accepted Nichols's version included a number of eulogizers who held Hickok entirely blameless for what happened, and inferred that he did the community a service in disposing of Dave, while the debunkers are adamant that he ambushed Tutt. The truth finally emerged when the original eyewitness statements made before the coroner were unearthed among the records of the Greene County Archive at Springfield.[3]

In summary, the eight witnesses gave their version of events under oath as follows:

Thomas D. Hudson said he was in Hursh's store when a man named Budlong came in and said that there was a difficulty on the square. The pair went along to see what it was and were in time to see Dave Tutt start out from the court house as "William Haycock" started to walk towards him from the other side of the square. Hudson saw Tutt go for his pistol, but instead of watching events he turned away and only heard the sound of a shot. He turned in time to see Tutt run back into the court house and then stagger out and collapse. He thought he only heard one pistol fired.

W.S. Riggs in a reference to the fatal card game on July 20, understood that Tutt claimed that Hickok owed him 35 dollars which Hickok denied, claiming that it was only 25. He had already paid him 10 dollars at "Oak Hall" [thought to be a gambling establishment that later became a clothing store]. Hickok had placed his watch on the table which Tutt picked up and said he would keep it until Hickok paid up. Wild Bill then

*Even before Tutt hit the ground, Hickok, according to Nichols, turned upon Dave's friends and asked them if they were satisfied or wished to continue the fight. (Courtesy **Harper's New Monthly Magazine,** February 1867.)*

offered to go down stairs and check his pocket book. But Tutt left asking Riggs to inform Hickok that if he paid him forty-five dollars he could have his watch. Riggs also reported that Hickok then asked John Orr to go to Tutt and tell him that he was ready at any time to pay him 25 dollars but no more unless his account book differed from his figures. Orr was also asked to return with the watch. On the day of the shoot-out, Riggs was on the square and saw Tutt start out from the court house while Hickok stepped out from the corner at the Robertson & Mason

store. He heard Hickok tell Tutt to stop as he wanted a settlement in regard to the watch. Riggs also heard them exchange other comments but was not close enough to learn what they were. He saw Tutt pull his pistol, but as Hickok's back was toward him, he did not see him draw his. However, he did see the smoke from Tutt's pistol and heard the sound of two shots. Hickok, he declared, was almost 100 yards away from Tutt when they opened fire. Tutt then ran around one of the pillers of the court house before collapsing near the door. Riggs also declared that he had

The Greene County Court-house at Springfield where Hickok's trial took place. Built in 1858, it was closed in 1912. Note the arches-- after he was shot, Dave staggered in one and out the other before collapsing on the square. (Author's collection.)

heard Hickok state that he believed Tutt would shoot him. He also heard Tutt declare that it would take a better man than Hickok to make him give up the watch.

John W. Orr in his evidence reviewed the dispute over the 35 dollars but added that he did not witness the shoot-out.

Lorenzo F. Lee declared that he was on the square on the evening of July 21 when he saw Hickok talking outside the Robertson and Mason store. He then turned and went onto the square. At that moment a man appeared wearing a white linen coat whom he did not recognize. Suddenly, he saw "the flash and smoke of two revolvers" and the man in the white coat ran into the court house and came out again and collapsed. "Saw the flash & smoke from the revolver of Haycock which he held in his hand, but did not see the revolver in the other man's hand, but saw the smoke & flash did not know which [who] fired first. Reports seemed to be simultaneous."

Eli Armstrong was on the square earlier on the evening of the 21st and was a friend of both Hickok and Tutt. He found Hickok, Tutt, and Orr sitting on the porch of the Lyon House. He asked what was the matter and learned of the disputed card game debt, and that Tutt now wanted $45. Armstrong took Tutt aside and advised him to accept 35 dollars and negotiate for the other ten, but Hickok was adamant that he only owed Tutt 25. Tutt then held up the watch and remarked that once he received 45 dollars Hickok could have his watch back. Hickok then said that he would rather have a "fuss with any man on earth than him for you have accom[m]odated me more than any man in town for I have

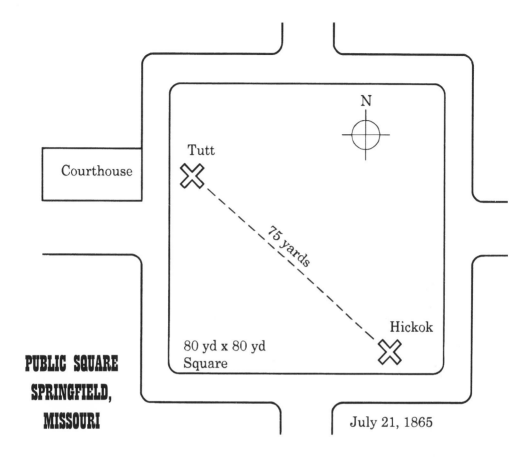

This sketch shows the positions of Hickok and Tutt on Public Square when they fired upon each other.

borrowed money from you time and again, and we have never had any dispute before in our settlement." Tutt agreed and said that he did not want trouble either. They all then went in for a drink but Tutt soon left, taking the watch with him. Armstrong then saw Tutt go to a livery stable and soon return. When he was about ten steps from the court house he heard Hickok call out advising Tutt not to cross the square with his watch. "Tutt made no reply but placed his hand on the butt of his Revolver. Tutt fired & so did Haycock but witness could not tell which [who] fired first[.] Tutt then turned round & placed his hand on his breast & said boys I am killed & ran into the Court House and fell at the door & rolled out on the ground at the door & died in about two minutes and perhaps not so long. Saw a bullet hole in his right side is satisfied both fired."

Oliver Scott agreed with much of

what Armstrong reported, but stated that Hickok told him that "the Tutts were all going for him." He did not witness the fight, but did hear the report of firearms.

A. L. Budlong's statement was very also similar to Armstrong's but he did not get a clear view of the fight. However, he was present when Dr. James stepped in and opened Tutt's vest and shirt and saw the wounds in Tutt's chest. He did not think Tutt fired, but he did notice an exploded cap on the nipple of Dave's pistol.

F. W. Scholten confirmed much of what the other witnesses had said; but added that one of Dave's brothers, John Tutt, had told Hickok that the family was sorry about the difficulty between Dave and himself and if he would come down Dave would settle it with him. Hickok then set out across the square to meet Dave. After the shooting Scholten turned to Hickok and remarked that it was rather hard, which Wild Bill said it was too late now and he was not sorry.

Dr. Edwin Ebert testified that when he examined Tutt's body he discovered that the bullet had "entered on the right side between the 5th and 7th rib and passed out on the left between the 5th and 7th rib[.] The examination being only superficial could not state the precise point[.] from his sudden death I am led to believe that some of the large

blood vessels were wounded." The bullet that killed Dave was never found.

Dr. Ebert's reference to Tutt's "sudden death" and his belief that "some of the large blood vessels were wounded" suggests that Hickok's bullet had passed through Tutt's heart. When we examine the witnesses' statements, however, it is clear that Dave remained on his feet for some moments and, according to Eli Armstrong, managed to gasp: "boys I am killed" before running into the court house and, emerging from the arches, falling on the ground and dying in about two minutes and perhaps not so long. Evidently, although Tutt drew first, both men fired together. Hickok, it will be recalled from Oliver Scott's statement, believed that all the Tutt family were against him.

The coroner's jury concluded that Davis K. Tutt came to his death from a pistol ball fired by the defendant, James B. Hickok, and he was remanded in custody to stand trial. Bail was set at $2,000 which was put up by a number of friends, among them Richard B. Owen and Isaac Hoff.

One curious feature of the Coroner's witness statements, however, is that only two of them (Eli Armstrong and L. F. Lee) saw both men open fire. The remainder heard

The Hickok-Tutt Gunfight

6:00 pm, July 21, 1865

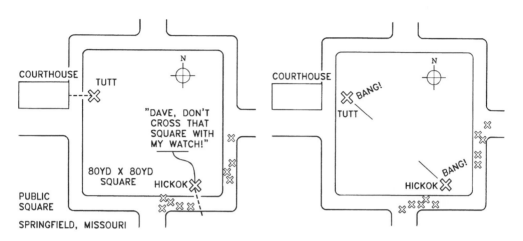

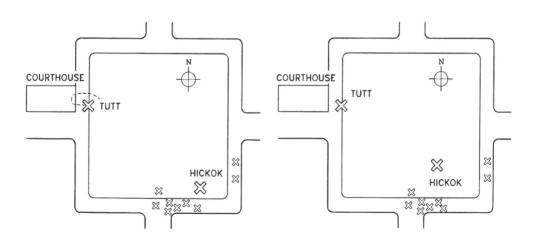

1. *July 21, 1865, 6:00 pm: Dave Tutt came from the courthouse onto the square when Hickok called out to him, "Dave, don't cross that square with my watch!" Friends and hangers-on had gathered to observe the confrontation.*

2. *6:00 pm: Dave Tutt reaches for his gun as does Hickok. Both fire at each other at the same time; both shots sounded as one shot. Dave misses but Hickok's 75 yard shot hits Dave in the chest.*

3. *6:01 pm: Dave Tutt grasps his chest, turns and runs to the entrance of the courthouse, circles one of its columns, and falls dead outside on the sidewalk.*

4. *6:03 pm: Moments after the shooting, Colonel Barnitz orders Hickok's arrest and he is handed over to the sheriff of Greene County.*

John S. Phelps in later life. He acted as Hickok's defense attorney, having known and employed Wild Bill during the late war. Owen had served as Phelp's quartermaster for a time. (Courtesy of Missouri Historical Society.)

the shots, or saw smoke or muzzle flash, while A. T. Budlong stated he "did not think Tutt fired," but admitted seeing his pistol with a discharged chamber.

The foregoing statements, however, make it clear that Nichols' version of events did him or his sources little credit, for instead of open enmity, it is now clear that neither Hickok nor Tutt were anxious to swap lead, and far from exchanging insults, they sought to avoid a shootout. For despite their dispute, they were friends—a point reiterated by Albert Barnitz. At the time of the shooting, Barnitz (who later served in Custer's Seventh Cavalry) was a colonel in the Second Ohio Volunteer Cavalry, and in command of the Post of Springfield. Within hours of the fight, he wrote in his journal that he had witnessed it and had ordered Hickok's arrest. He stated that both men fired together, and confirmed that they had been "intimate for years and have been gambling together to-day [*sic*]. The ill will seems to have originated at the gambling table."[4]

A much disputed facet of the Hickok-Tutt encounter is the distance between both men when they opened fire. Colonel George Ward Nichols gives it as both fifty paces and fifty yards. Colonel Barnitz, however, says the distance was "100 paces," while other witnesses suggested that the distance was between 100 and 120 paces. In recent years, local historians who consulted early maps and measured the distance between both combatants, concluded that the actual distance was 75 yards. But the most remarkable feature of the shoot-out was discovered when we examined the previously cited coroner's report and the examination of Dave's wounds. This disclosed that Dave was facing Hickok side-on—duelling fashion—when shots were exchanged, which adds further credence to Hickok's ability as a pistol shot.

Hickok's trial opened on August 5, 1865, and among the many documents that came to light was the original Indictment for Manslaughter. Hickok was charged as "William Haycocke," and Tutt was named as "David Tutt." Later, during the trial, Hickok's attorney (John S. Phelps who had employed Hickok at one time as a scout during the late war) had the indictment amended so that the names "William Haycocke"" and "David Tutt" were changed to "James B. Hickock" and "Davis K. Tutt" respectively. Among the court records is a reference to Tutt as "Little Dave" which was not meant to be demeaning, but was a term in use before the more familiar "junior" became common to indicate that one was named after one's father or a relative.

In reviewing the evidence, one is left with the impression that Tutt's refusal to accept Hickok's offer of a partial settlement, with the promise of more if his pocket book confirmed the amount, suggests that perhaps there was another dispute between the pair that was not publicized. But I am not convinced that it had anything to do with a woman as was hinted at by "Captain Honesty," and his suggestion that Hickok was forced to fight rather than give up "his honor" is romantic, but it does not resolve the problem. Therefore, I wonder if it had anything to do with Tutt's brush with the law the day before the shoot-out?

Dave's troubles began back in December, 1864, when he was charged with illegal gambling and resisting arrest. He appeared in court on July 20, 1865, and was fined $100 and costs. Unable to pay up, he was jailed. Thomas G. Martin, Hickok's erstwhile scouting "mate" then came to his rescue and arranged his release. Much later, Martin was called to account for monies still owed to the court from Tutt's estate. These facts might explain why Dave was so anxious to get money from Wild Bill, or indeed any source. But if this was the case, surely he could have explained the situation to Hickok—who after all was his friend and in the past had been indebted to him—and

The grave of Dave Tutt at the Maple Park Cemetery in Springfield, Missouri. (Courtesy of Robert Neumann and photographer Amy Langston, Greene County Archives, Springfield, Missouri.)

the pair could have reached a compromise? If indeed there was another reason, then perhaps it may never be revealed—but stranger things have happened!

It is noticeable that the court records all name him as Wm. Haycocke or Haycock, J. B. Hickok or Hickock. Although Hickok was known to most of his acquaintances as "Bill" (from as early as 1857), none of the documents so far examined described him as "Wild Bill"—it was the *Weekly Missouri Patriot* of July 27 which stated that James B. Hickok was better known in South-West Missouri as "Wild Bill," and is believed to be the first printed reference to his sobriquet.

Finally, one other facet of the Tutt case needs to be reexamined. This concerns the statement published in the *Weekly Missouri Patriot* of Au-

gust 10, 1865, which was highly critical of Hickok. The editor intimated that it was the Judge's opinion and that the jury angered public opinion by rendering a "Not Guilty" verdict. However, when the original court records were examined, I discovered that the *Patriot* published the prosecutor's summing up to the jury and not those of the judge. Had Judge Boyd's summing up been cited, then perhaps much of the controversy surrounding the fight might have been dispelled.

The judge was quite specific in his remarks, pointing out that if the jury believed that Tutt advanced on Hickok with a drawn pistol and that he had previously made threats of violence toward him, and his knowledge that Tutt was a "fighting character & a dangerous man," Hickok would have had reason enough to believe that his life was threatened. If the jury accepted that Hickok acted in self-defense, for "when danger threatened and impending a man is not compelled to stand with his arms folded until it is too late to offer successful resistance," he would be entitled to defend himself.

The jury, influenced more by Judge Boyd's instructions than those of the prosecuting counsel, Mr. Fyan, took just ten minutes to find Hickok "Not Guilty."

In hindsight, of course, the Hickok-Tutt fight could have been avoided had Dave Tutt accepted Hickok's word that he genuinely believed that he did not owe him $35 dollars, but only $25. And had Tutt needed the money to get out of debt—something he could have mentioned at the time—it might have saved his life; but perhaps pride came first. And, perhaps, Hickok could have resolved the situation had he produced his pocket book or memorandum as soon as the dispute arose. Indeed, some might suggest that he had no such record and was stalling, and others that had Dave not provoked Hickok over the watch the matter would probably have been resolved amicably. In the circumstances, the Hickok-Tutt fight was more a tragic confrontation than a premeditated gunfight.

This shootout remains as one of the few stand-up, face-to-face, duel-type gunfights of the gunfighting era. It was a fair fight where both participants retained their honor.

Notes

1. Charles F. Gross to J. B. Edwards, June 15, 1925, Manuscripts Department Kansas State Historical Society.

2. For an annotated version of the original Nichols article, *see* Joseph G. Rosa, "George Ward Nichols and the Legend of Wild Bill Hickok," *Arizona and the West* (Summer 1977).

3. Joseph G. Rosa, "Little Dave's Last Fight: What Really Happened when Wild Bill Hickok and Davis K. Tutt Shot it out at Springfield, Missouri," National Association For Outlaw and Lawman History's *Quarterly* (October-December, 1996), 3-15.

4. Major Albert Barnitz, Diary and Journals covering the period 1861-1870. (Barnitz Papers, the Benecke Library, Yale University).

Chapter Six

HAYS CITY:
THE MULVEY AND STRAWHUN SHOOTOUTS

Hays City, Kansas, when it was established on August 23, 1867, by William E. Webb, an officer and agent of the Big Creek Land Company, consisted of a couple of shacks and some tents built on land purchased from the Union Pacific Railway Company (Eastern Division). Located about half a mile from the small town of Rome, speculation was rife whether the tracks of the railroad would pass through Hays or Rome.

Probably because it was built on land ceded by the U.P.E.D., the company decided on Hays City, and it remained an end-of-track town until the railroad moved on to Sheridan en route for Denver. Sited about a mile from Fort Hays, within weeks the place had mushroomed and acquired a formidable reputation and where, according to the Leavenworth *Daily Conservative* of September 29, nobody "sits down to a social game of cards without laying a revolver upon the table and loosening his bowie knife in its sheath. The place is reported to be similar to California in '49. If reports are true, they must be 'real purty' places to live in." This opinion was enhanced when the post commander at Fort Hays stationed an NCO and six soldiers in town to act as a guard. According to the Lawrence *Kansas Daily Tribune* of November 26, a visitor complained that the place was "really under martial law," and what made it "trebly obnoxious to some, the soldiers are colored." However, it was agreed that they maintained "quiet and good order throught out the day and night."

During the next five years Hays continued to have an unenviable reputation as the haunt of soldiers, buffalo hunters, prostitutes, cardsharps and, toward the end of its violent period, it was described as "a row of saloons" alongside the railroad, a veritable "Sodom of the Plains."

*Wild Bill circa 1869-70 at the time he was acting sheriff and a deputy U.S. Marshal at Hays City. This image appeared as a woodcut in Webb's **Buffalo Land** and is believed to be one of at least two poses made at the same sitting. A full-face version is credited to James H. Leonard of Topeka which suggests that he also made this plate. (Courtesy the Kansas State Historical Society.)*

This enlargement of the photograph at the right gives a better view of Hickok.

Later, Hickok included it in his widely reported comment that there was "no Sunday west of Junction City, no law west of Hays City, and no God west of Carson City."[1]

Evidently, Hays City's awesome reputation did not bother Wild Bill, for he made the place his headquarters from late in 1867 until December 1869, during which time he was in and out of the town on official business as a policeman, an army scout, acting sheriff or as a deputy U.S.

Marshal. Late in December 1867 he built and operated a saloon. This was located on south Fort Street (now 9th street), and he was reported to be running it as late as June 1868. From August 1868 until February 1869, Hickok was again in the service of the government as a scout. He returned to Hays City late in April 1869 following a visit to his mother's home in Illinois. He found Hays City to be without any official law enforcement following several months of near an-

Alexander Gardner reached Fort Harker late in September 1867, where he photographed a large group of men in the Quartermaster's department. The Quartermaster, Colonel Henry Inman is centered, while Wild Bill (at that time a deputy U.S. Marshal) is the extreme left. His two Colt's Navy pistols are prominenently displayed. (Author's collection.)

archy at the hands of Black troops of the 38th Infantry stationed at Fort Hays, and the innumerable "roughs" who frequented the many saloons and brothels.

Hays City's early reputation for violence received nationwide attention which soon attracted visitors, many of them tourists. Although most were favorable, there were some whose remarks were made safer by distance. Among these was the previously mentioned E. W.

Halford of the Indianapolis *Journal* whose comments on Hays City and its residents angered them. In a letter to the editor of the *Leavenworth Daily Commercial* published on August 3, 1869, Michael Joyce, in recalling Halford's earlier low life career as a saloon-keeper on the Cleveland, Ohio, waterfront, quoted the following comments on Hickok from the article:

Here we saw "Wild Bill," the famous scout, made notorious through the articles published about his life in *Harper's Magazine*. He is rather a young looking man, with a light moustache, curved nose, and hair curling down over his shoulders. Blue eyes and a parchment colored skin make up anything but an attractive looking face, although Bill evidently prides himself as being a "stunner." He wears his pistols cocked, walks in his shirt sleeves, and is the standing terror of cross little children, and the *ultima* of the admiration of the women of the village. His proper name[,] he told me[,] was J. B. Hickok, and his weight two hundred and four pounds, though his appearance would not place it above one hundred and seventy-five.

The time at our disposal did not permit any extended talk, but from what we saw of him, we were of the opinion that he is a braggart and a coward. If a firm man got hold of him he would cowe, and fight like a rat, when it is impossible for him to run. The station agent told us that there were three or four men in Hays to whom Bill gives a very wide berth.

The idea of Hickok walking around with two *cocked* pistols and the possibility of a misfire is ludicrous—presumably Halford meant he wore them in a state of readiness. Joyce ignored that point, but was quick to defend Wild Bill: "I wish to state that there is not, nor never has been a more quiet and peaceable citizen than J. B. Hickok," and Halford's allegation that the station agent (J. W. Perrie) fed him stories about Hickok and others was a fabrication and an "injustice" to Mr. Perrie. However biased, truthful or inaccurate such comments might be, they are grist to the mill of make-believe that enhances or besets the reputation of anyone in the public eye.

As for Hays, from its very beginning, law and order was at best tenuous. Ellis County was organized on October 28, 1867, by Governor Samuel J. Crawford, and Hays City became its temporary seat. Thomas Gannon was elected sheriff on December 5, and at the first meeting of the Ellis County Commissioners held on January 6, 1868, he was authorized to employ two "policemen" to be paid $70 a month. These appointments were evidently intended to police Hays City and the declining hamlet of Rome. In February Wes T. Butler and Peter R. Lanihan were appointed policemen and each paid $75 per month. Some believe that Sheriff Gannon disappeared from Hays early in 1868—killed from ambush according to several accounts. But from available evidence it seems he may have simply resigned and moved on, the most likely reason being that he had not been paid (Ellis County

Samuel O. Strawhun who fell victim to Wild Bill's marksmanship during the night of September 26-27, 1869. (Courtesy Mrs. Jean Fisherkeller.)

finances are a subject outside the scope of this study), in his place was acting Sheriff John V. Macintosh. Following Hays City's incorporation on February 6, 1868, another policeman, Rufus Edwards, was added to the police force, and on February 17, Isaac Thayer was appointed as city marshal and served until April 8, 1868.

On August 15, 1868, Lanihan and Edwards resigned, which technically left Hays City already without a marshal, in the guardian care of several township constables who would remain in office until the April 1869 elections. Isaac Thayer, meantime

was still in the vicinity. In August 1868 he was one of the men who volunteered for Forthsyth's Scouts who won fame at Beecher Island. On his return to Hays he stood for sheriff and was elected on November 3, 1868. By May 1869, he, too, had disappeared, but later surfaced in 1871 at Newton where he was involved in the Gold Room.[2]

Hickok, meanwhile, during his sporadic appearances in Hays City, was kept busy. In May 1869 he was ordered to Fort Wallace to escort prisoners of the U.S. Marshal to Topeka. Some claim that he was elected as City Marshal (or as a policeman) at

This photograph of Wild Bill is credited to J. Lee Knight of Topeka, Kansas, but he appears to have copied an existing and damaged print. The original plate may have been made by Charles T. Smith of Topeka or perhaps E.E. Henry of Leavenworth, circa 1867-69. Hickok sports only one Navy pistol worn butt forward for a cross body draw. The belt buckle appears identical to that worn in the photograph made at Fort Harker. (Courtresy Randall Deihl.)

the Big Creek township elections held on April 6, but this is unlikely because he was known to be in Illinois at the time visiting his family. The successful candidate was probably Peter Lanihan who had served as a policeman the previous year. Ellis County now had no sheriff and Hays City was without a city marshal, and continued to rely upon township policemen to preserve what order they could.[3]

On July 7, 1869, two months after Sheriff Thayer disappeared, and still without an effective police force, the citizens of Hays petitioned the governor to appoint one R. A. Eccles as sheriff. The governor ignored their request, and some suspect this was because he was concerned over Thayer's disappearance. Meanwhile, the controversial vigilance committee made no secret of its likes and dislikes. Among those who offended it were saloon-keeper Joseph Weiss and Samuel Strawhun. Mr. Weiss, was a former inmate of the State Penitentiary; an unsuccessful candidate for sheriff at the November 1868 election, and a former deputy U.S. Marshal, while Mr. Strawhun was a familiar figure as a teamster at Fort Hays, or in and around the various saloons. Late in July, when it was decided that both men should leave town, Alonzo B. Webster, the postal clerk, and an active member of the vigilance committee, was given the unenviable task of advising the pair that they must leave. Instead, Weiss and Strawhun decided to confront him and invaded the Post Office. The *Junction City Union* of July 31, 1869, citing the Leavenworth *Commercial*, reported that the pair "abused, slapped, and finally drew a revolver upon Webster, who was too quick for them," and grabbed a pistol and mortally wounded Weiss with a shot "through the bowels." Strawhun then fired a shot at him through the window and fled, but soon returned with some friends anxious for revenge. According to an obituary for Webster published in the *Ford County Republican* of April 20, 1887, Strawhun found Hickok seated on the counter, and Hickok advised them that he was prepared to take over the fight. They fled. Two months later Strawhun had his own encounter with Wild Bill.

Webster's later career included a period as the mayor of Dodge City, where his activities against saloon-keepers and gamblers made him many enemies. When he cast aspersions against Jack Downing, the editor of the *Ellis County Star,* Downing was quick to respond. In his issue of February 17, 1881, he inferred that perhaps Webster's killing of Weiss was not the reaction of a man scared out of his wits, but calculated, adding: "Now let us assure Mr. Webster—since he has associated us with men classed as murderers—that it is not out of any respect we entertain for him, but from a very high regard we have for others, that the killing of Joe Weise [*sic*], on the streets of this City some years ago, is not made part of this article."

The governor's rejection of their petition of July 7 made the citizens more determined to have law and order, and their actions, and those of the County Commissioners (aided by the vigilance committee) remain controversial. The County Commissioners, relying upon existing Kansas Statutes, deemed it legal (because there was no under sheriff) to organize an election to provide an acting sheriff pending the forthcoming official election in November. This met with the approval of the vigilance committee. When this was held in

August, Hickok was elected as acting sheriff of Ellis County, and others were elected to fill various city vacancies. The Topeka *Commonwealth* of September 5 in its coverage of the election stated that "whenever the 'roughs' want a particular man in office, if they can gain their point in no other way, they hold a 'special election' and go through the farce of electing him." The governor shared that view, and declared the election illegal. The County Commissioners were adamant, pointing out that they were guided by existing statutes.

Later, the governor realized that they had a point, and, in January 1870, he asked the state legislature to amend the law so that only the governor could appoint a sheriff in the event that there was no under sheriff to complete an existing term. Historian James Drees has found some evidence that following the April 1869 election, Hays City suffered a period of disincorporation, which meant that both town constables and the county sheriff would be responsible for law enforcement. Therefore, despite the governor's protests, between August and December 1869, when Wild Bill drew his pistols to preserve law and order, or to defend himself for the first time since his shoot-out with Davis K. Tutt four years earlier, he did so in the belief that he was acting in a legal capacity.

There is, however, confusion over the exact date of the election. Most sources give the date as August 23, but the Leavenworth *Times and Conservative* of August 22, in a report dated Hays City August 18, stated that Hickok was already acting in an official capacity and was unable to house his prisoners (although Hays City did possess a jail of sorts). This suggests that perhaps prior to the election, Hickok was employed as a policeman, which would account for the undated document presented on his behalf to Ellis County for $122.50 in payment for one month and 19 days for "services as a policeman."

Although it might refer to an earlier period (1868?), if it was for service rendered prior to the election, it would explain his right to step in when violence erupted within the city, as indeed he did when Bill Mulvey (or Mulrey) and several drunken cronies started to shoot up the town. The Atchison *Patriot* on the 24th reported that Hickok shot him on the 22nd, the day before the election for sheriff is believed to have taken place. The Lawrence *Tribune* of August 26, citing the Leavenworth *Commercial,* declared that Mulvey was "determined to quarrel with everyone whom he met, using his revolver freely, but fortunately injur-

South Main Street of Hays City, Kansas in 1868. (Courtesy of Kansas State Historical Society.)

ing no one." Hickok at first tried to persuade him to disarm, and when that failed, he drew his own pistol and opened fire. Legendary accounts of the incident suggest that Hickok diverted his attention long enough to convince him that someone behind him was about to open fire. The *North Topeka Times* of August 31, 1876, claimed that Hickok did indeed distract him and that when Mulvey turned his head, Wild Bill shot him, "the bullet having entered just back of the right ear."

Other reports, however, published at the time of the shooting, among them the Kansas City *Daily Journal of Commerce*, of August 25 claimed that Wild Bill shot him "through the neck and lungs." He was still alive when the paper was published, but died shortly afterwards. This shooting and Hickok's purported actions inspired similar ploys in novels and numerous Hollywood Westerns.

Understandably, pro- and anti-Hickok writers still argue over the implications of both descriptions—was he facing Hickok when Wild Bill fired, or was he shot in the back of the head? At this late date, without the benefit of the coroner's report or independent witnesses, no one can provide an accurate account of how Mulvey died. But insofar as the citizens of Hays City were concerned, his death was no great loss to mankind, and we must not lose sight of the fact that Hickok and his kind did not survive gunfights by being chivalrous—being "quick or dead" meant just that: every advantage, short of back shooting or killing an unarmed man, counted when confronted by someone homicidally inclined in your direction. Indeed, the subject of survival among the gunfighting elite was ably described in the Topeka *Daily Commonwealth* of December 6, 1871, which declared that "such men as Wild Bill who fight with the weapons best adapted to the circumstances almost invariably carry the day, even in the face of immense odds."

Writing in *The Galaxy* magazine in 1872 (and published in book form in 1874 as *My Life on the Plains*), General George A. Custer expressed a similar opinion. In describing Hickok's practice of carrying a pair of ivory-handled revolvers, he remarked that:

> Where this is the common custom, brawls or personal difficulties are seldom if ever settled by blows. The quarrel is not from a word to a blow, but from a word to the revolver, and he who can draw and fire first is the best man. No civil law reaches him; none is applied for. In fact there is no law recognized beyond the frontier but that of "might makes right."

Should death result from the quarrel, as it usually does, no coroner's jury is impaneled to learn the cause of death, and the survivor is not arrested. But instead of these old-fashioned proceedings, a meeting of citizens takes place, the survivor is *requested* to be present when the circumstances of the homicide are inquired into, and the unfailing verdict of "justifiable," "self-defense," etc., is pronounced, and the law stands vindicated. That justice is often deprived of a victim there is not a doubt. Yet in all the many affairs of this kind in which "Wild Bill" has performed a part, and which have come to my knowledge, there is not a single instance in which the verdict of twelve fair-minded men would not be pronounced in his favor.

The controversy surrounding Hickok's election as acting sheriff of Ellis County ignores the fact that either he or the County Commissioners later appointed a deputy. This deputy was Peter R. Lanihan (sometimes spelled Lanahan), the former policeman who made rare appearances in the record during Hickok's tenure in office until he himself achieved an official status later in the year. The first mention of his involvement with Wild Bill came on the night of September 27 when Hickok was called on to intervene in an ugly

This view of North Main Street of Hays City is circa 1879, some years after Wild Bill's departure, but it is interesting because it depicts the famous New York House hotel where Hickok stayed on occasion. In the center of the photograph and marked with an "X" is Tommy Drum's saloon. Here, according to several sources, Hickok and Jim Curry, restaurant owner, part-time pimp, and former engineer on the Union Pacific Railway (Eastern Division) once had a near fatal encounter for an undisclosed reason.

Curry, according to old-timer Tom Ranahan was the only man who Hickok "dreaded" simply because he was totally unpredictable. Consequently, when Curry came up behind Hickok as he sat in Drum's saloon, and thrust a pistol in his ear and roared, "Now, you son of a gun! I've got you!" Hickok's cold-blooded poker-faced reaction made Curry hesitate. "Now, Jim, you would not murder a man without giving him a show." "I'll give you the same show you would give me, you long-haired tough!" roared Curry. "Jim, let us settle this feud. How would a bottle of champagne all round do?" The crowd erupted in laughter and broke the tension. Both men shook hands and the feud was over. (Courtesy Kansas State Historical Society.)

situation precipitated by Strawhun and his cronies. As was the Mulvey incident, Hickok's confrontation with Strawhun would be controversial.

Samuel O. Strawhun (whose name was sometimes spelled Strawhan, Stringham, and other variations) was born in Missouri in 1845, and some members of his family were still living at Rolla, Missouri, in the late 1860s. Sam was well known in Hays City, where most of the time he was usefully employed by the military as a teamster or courier. Early in March, 1869, however, deputy U.S. Marshal John S. Park arrested him on a Federal warrant sworn out by U.S. Commissioner Milton W. Soule and placed him in the Fort Hays guardhouse.

The record does not explain why he was arrested; but it has been suggested that Strawhun was at one time a member of the John Donovan horse-stealing gang which ranked among its members Jack Ledford, John Sanderson, and other desperate characters well known in Kansas. William E. Connelley in his *Wild Bill and his Era* claimed that in 1867, working out of Fort Riley, Hickok, at the head of a company of scouts, was responsible for the recovery of more than two hundred horses and mules from the Solomon Valley, but he did not return with any prisoners. He claimed that Hickok was a Deputy U.S. Marshal; but records disclose that from January 1866 until May 1867, Hickok was employed as a government detective, which would have given him the authority to undertake such a mission (which has not been verified). Whether Strawhun was a member of a gang of horse thieves has not been proved, but Connelley told A. J. Bellport, one of Hickok's fiercest critics, that Strawhun was involved.[4]

Sam Strawhun was also one of the signatories to the petition that was sent to the governor requesting that he appoint Eccles as acting sheriff; but for some reason he incurred the wrath of the vigilance committee that led to the shootout between Joe Weiss and Alonzo Webster. Sam kept a low profile following that fracas, and it was claimed that Hickok himself had warned him to change his base. But late in September, he and a number of cronies or "wolves" (many of them friends of the late Joe Weiss) decided it was their night to howl.

Late in the evening of September 26th they invaded the John Bitter's Beer Saloon on Fort Street. Mr. Bitter, it has been alleged, was also a member of the vigilance committee, which may explain why they chose his place to raise a ruckus. By the early hours of the morning of the 27th, a large number of his beer glasses had been removed to a vacant lot next door amid threats to anyone who tried to retrieve them.

Bitter sent someone to find Wild Bill, and when he and Deputy Lanihan arrived they quickly assessed the situation. Hickok personally went out to the vacant lot and gathered up a number of glasses and deposited them on the bar. Lanihan, evidently took no further part in the action that followed.

J. W. Buel claimed that Hickok was standing at the bar staring into the mirror when Strawhun came up behind him with a levelled revolver.

Wild Bill calmly drew one of his own pistols and, thrusting the barrel over his left shoulder, shot Sam through the head.

Why Hickok should be staring into a mirror when the place was in uproar was not explained, and adds nothing to our knowledge of the situation. Neither do comments from old-timers who claimed fifty and sixty years later to have been there. Writing in 1929, A. D. Bellport alleged that "Sam was shot in the back of the head without having been given a chance for his life." Unfortunately, he destroyed his credibility by alleging that the citizens of Hays were so terrified of Wild Bill that no one dared to oppose him, which of course is ridiculous. But if he really had a grudge or evidence against Hickok, why did he wait almost sixty years to divulge it?[5]

Bellport's allegation was not shared by the press. Statewide reports confirmed that Sam and his companions were indeed on a "spree" and, according to the Junction City *Weekly Union* of October 2, were determined to "clean out a beer saloon." In "quieting the disturbance Wild Bill shot him, which quieted the disturbance, so far as Strangham was concerned."

Some reports claimed that Sam had made some disparaging remarks against Wild Bill, but they were not recorded. Instead, Hickok's handling of the affair was of greater concern. The Lawrence *Daily Tribune* of September 30 declared that Hickok, in his "efforts to preserve order" shot Strawhun "through the head" and he died instantly. "Justice [M. E.] Joyce held an inquest on the body today [27th], six well-known citizens being selected for the jurymen. The evidence in one or two instances was very contradictory. The jury returned a verdict to the effect that Samuel Stringham came to his death from a pistol wound at the hands of J. B. Hickok, and that the shooting of said Stringham was justifiable." The Leavenworth *Times and Conservative* of September 28 agreed: "It appears that Strangham and a number of his companions being 'wolfing' all night, wished to conclude by cleaning out a beer saloon and breaking things generally. 'Wild Bill' was called upon to quiet them. In the melee that followed Strangham was killed. The Coroner's verdict this morning [27th] was justifiable homicide. Stranghan was buried this afternoon."

According to the Wichita *Eagle* of September 14, 1876, John Malone, who had known Hickok for some years and in later life was a state senator, said that when Hickok reached the saloon and realized how serious the situation was, he tried to ease tension. "Boys, you hadn't ought

The Hickok-Strawhun Fight

September 27, 1869
Hays City, Kansas

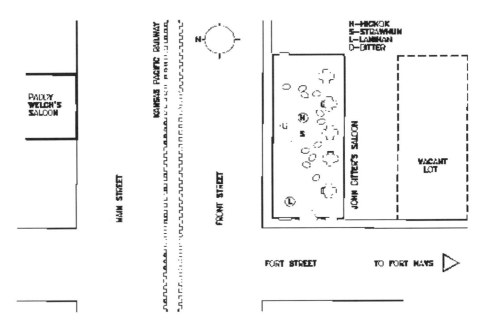

John Bitter's Beer Saloon was typical of the early saloon--a narrow front with a lengthy interior. This drawing depicts the moment at which Hickok shot Strawhun after having visited the vacant lot to retrieve empty beer glasses.

to treat a poor old man in this way," he said. Strawhun retorted that he would throw the glasses out again. "Do," Hickok replied, "and they will carry you out."

The most graphic account of the incident, by an unnamed eyewitness dated Hays City September 30, was published in the Leavenworth *Daily Commercial* on October 3, 1869:

It seems that there was on the part of this Stranhan and some of his associates bad feeling against certain citizens of this town, and members of the Vigilance committee. To satisfy their hatred they mobbed together and went on Sunday night, about half-past 11 o'clock to the saloon of Mr. John Bitter, with the intent to break up the establishment. The crowd, numbering about fourteen to eighteen persons, called for beer in a frantic manner. The glasses had to

The Hickok-Strawhun Fight

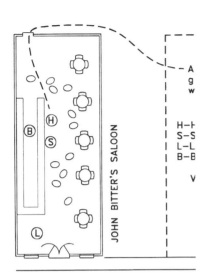

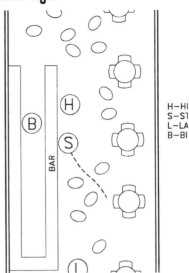

1. September 27, 1869, 1:30 am: Hickok picks up the empty glasses from the vacant lot, takes them inside, and places them on the bar.

2. 1:31 am: An angry Strawhun approaches Hickok and says that he intends to kill anyone who interferes with his fun. Strawhun picks up a glass from the bar.

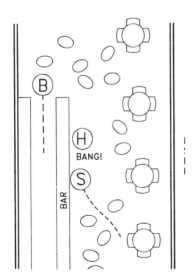

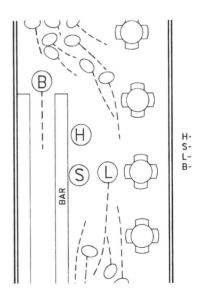

3. 1:31 am: Strawhun approaches Hickok with empty beer mug in a threatening manner. Hickok draws his pistol, shoots, and kills Strawhun.

4. 1:32 am: Strawhun falls to the floor and his band of a dozen or so cohorts disperse as the gunsmoke settles.

be filled up continually. Meanwhile the men were passing in and out of the saloon, and as it afterwards appeared carried the glasses to an adjoining vacant lot. Mr. Bitter remarked that the number of glasses was diminishing, and saw that Stranhan carried out some of them.

The noise was fearful, all the men crying at the top of their voices, beer! beer! and using the most obscene language. This went on for a short time, when they began throwing the beer at each other. During all the noise one could hear threats as: "I shall kill someone to-night just for luck," or "some one will have to go up to-night," etc.

Mr. Bitter finally called the policeman [*sic*], Mr. Wm. Hickock, known as "Wild Bill," asking him to go out and fetch the missing glasses back. Wild Bill shortly returned with both hands full of glasses, when Strawhan remarked that he would shoot anyone that should try to interfere with his fun. Wild Bill set the glasses on the counter, Stranhan took hold of one and took it up in a threatening manner. He had no time to exercise his design for a shot fired by Mr. Hickock killed him. He dropped down dead.

The inquest was held next morning at 9 o'clock. The verdict of the jury was that deceased was shot by Mr. Hickock, and that the homicide was justifiable, the same being in self-defense. Too much credit cannot be given to Wild Bill for his endeavor to rid this town of such dangerous characters as this Stranham was.

Much of the controversy surrounding this fight centers upon whether Hickok was threatened by a man wielding a beer glass or a six-shooter. A pacifist once tried hard to convince me that Hickok reacted in panic; but blanched when I described to him the horrific injuries which could be sustained by having a broken and jagged beer bottle or glass jabbed into one's face.

If that is what really happened (remember Hickok was surrounded by a hostile crowd), it is not surprising that his actions were accepted by the coroner's jury. Only Buel thought it more romantic to include a mirror, presumably in an attempt to further romanticize Hickok's dexterity with firearms.

Hickok's tenure in Hays City came to an end following the November election when his deputy, Democrat Peter Lanihan, was elected sheriff and assumed his duties in January 1870. On December 24, Hickok, in his role as a deputy U. S. Marshal, arrested one John Adams accused of stealing government livestock for personal profit. By the end of the year, however, Wild Bill had moved to Topeka and also spent some of his time at Junction City. During the early months of 1870 he visited friends in Warrensburg and Jefferson City, Missouri, where he caused a sensation on the floor of the House when invited to meet the Legislature.

In July, however, he was back in Hays City. Whether this visit was personal or in his guise as a deputy U.S. Marshal is uncertain, for he was involved in a shoot-out with two, possibly more, members of the Seventh Cavalry that has become a classic, and like so many incidents in Hickok's career, myth soon displaced fact.

Notes

1. Wichita (Kansas) *Weekly Beacon*, October 28, 1874, crediting its original appearance to the Boston *Journal*. However, the St. Louis *Daily Democrat* of March 5, 1873, used the quote to presage an attack on violence in the Far West.

2. James D. Drees, *Bloody Prairie: Ellis County's Wildest Years 1865-1875* (Hays, Kansas, 1997), Vol. II, 22-26; James D. Drees to Joseph G. Rosa, July 4, 1999.

3. James D. Drees to Joseph G. Rosa, April 10, 1999. Mr. Drees has had access to all available early records of Ellis County, which he has supplemented by a close examination of statewide and outside newspapers and other sources. Hickok's account for services as a "policeman" penned by a clerk or another official, was presented to the Kansas State Historical Society in 1882.

4. Drees, *Bloody Prairie, loc. cit.* Little of Connelley's source material is known today; but there is a large collection devoted to Hickok and Quantrill in the Western History Department of the Denver Public Library.

5. A. D. Bellport to G. W. Hansen, March 15, 1929, Manuscripts Department, Nebraska State Historical Society, Lincoln, Neb. Had Hickok displayed the terrorizing tactics suggested by Bellport, it would have led to his arrest not exoneration.

Chapter Seven

HAYS CITY:
THE FIGHT WITH 7TH CAVALRY SOLDIERS

Wild Bill's appearance at Hays City in July 1870, nearly cost him his life. On the evening of July 17 he was in John D. Walsh's saloon, with his back to the room, talking to the bartender when two Seventh Cavalry troopers entered. "Paddy Welch's" place as it was generally called, was popular with troops and citizens alike, which might explain why little attention was paid to Jeremiah Lonergan and John Kile. Lonergan was known as a troublemaker, and Kile, a deserter recently re-inducted into the Seventh, had previously served with the Fifth Cavalry where he was awarded the Congressional Medal of Honor for his actions in protecting his companions in an Indian skirmish the previous year.

It is ironic, therefore, that someone who was prepared to sacrifice himself for his companions should be remembered only as a drunken, brawling thug.

Predictably, press reports of what happened that evening, and the number of troopers involved, are mixed and contradictory. The Topeka, Kansas, *Daily Commonwealth* of July 22 claimed that "Five soldiers attacked Bill," and that the "sentiment of the community is with 'Bill,' as it is claimed he but acted in self-defense."

The Junction City *Union* of the 23rd, named the two soldiers as "Langan and Kelly," adding that the "greatest excitement prevails in the town owing to the outrage." Following the shootout, Wild Bill "made for the prairie and has not been heard of since. The citizens were out en masse looking for Bill, so that he might be summarily dealt with. The parties were all under the influence of liquor at the time." The Clyde *Re-*

publican Valley Empire on August 2, however, described the affair as a "friendly scuffle" between Hickok and a soldier which ended in a row. Only when another soldier intervened did he shoot and mortally wound one of them and leave "for parts unknown."

Another version of events which extols Wild Bill's dexterity with a pistol rather than fact, and perhaps owes its origin more to Buel than recorded fact, was described by old-time buffalo hunter Matt Clarkson, an early day resident of Hays City who recorded his recollections in his old age:

Wild Bill got into trouble with some soldiers in Tommy Drum's saloon [*sic*]. He drew two sixshooters and begun [*sic*] firing, backing toward the door, when he got outside two other soldiers begun firing at him from behind, so he kept the fellows in front covered with his left hand and threw his right hand over his right shoulder shot backward and killed another soldier. He realized what he had done and thought he had better leave. His horse was tied behind the saloon. He jumped on him and started north. In thirty minutes a bunch of soldiers started in persuit[*sic*]. When Bill got to North Fork he turned down the creek. The soldiers thot [*sic*— thought] he had gone north to Stockton. Bill went on down to a wood choppers camp, where he had his wounds bound, and stayed in camp about a week. . . .

Curiously, Clarkson's claim that Hickok headed to North Fork (renamed Victoria) received some support from C. J. Bascom who said he was there when Hickok came through, claiming to be looking for horse thieves. He was given a meal before moving on, and when an officer accompanied by four privates drove up in a Fort Hays ambulance, Bascom denied all knowledge of Wild Bill or his whereabouts. The soldiers left, but Bascom heard the officer remark: "that man knows more than he cares to tell."[1]

Why, one may well ask, did the troopers attack Hickok? Stories of a feud between Hickok and some members of the Seventh are not borne out by any known records. Therefore, are we to assume that Hickok spent some time drinking with the soldiers which led to the fight, or did they attack him for another reason? It has been suggested that Lonergan and Kile went AWOL that evening which made them deserters in military eyes. If Hickok was indeed in Hays City in his capacity as a deputy U.S. Marshal, then he could have arrested the pair and claimed a reward. But to do that he would have needed prior notification that they were wanted men. It was John Ryan, (a sergeant in the

The Fight With 7th Cavalry Soldiers

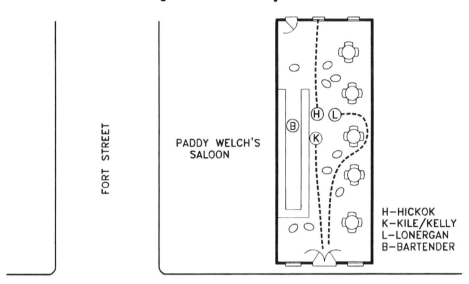

FORT STREET

PADDY WELCH'S
SALOON

H—HICKOK
K—KILE/KELLY
L—LONERGAN
B—BARTENDER

MAIN STREET

KANSAS PACIFIC RAILWAY

FRONT STREET

N

TO FORT HAYS

JOHN BITTER'S SALOON

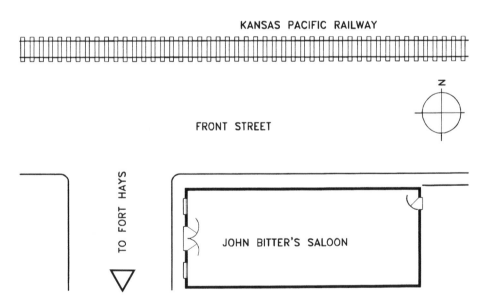

Paddy Welch's saloon on the evening of July 17-18, 1870. No reliable sources have divulged how many people were present when Lonergan decided to attack Hickok. Neither is it known if the three had been drinking before the event. However, if Sergeant Ryan is correct, the attack on Hickok was unprovoked, and this layout shows the moment when Lonergan came up behind Hickok and grabbed him.

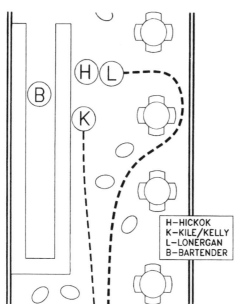

1. *July 17, 1870, 9:15 pm: Lonergan surprised Hickok from behind, pinned his arms to his side, and wrestled him to the floor, as Kile joins him.*

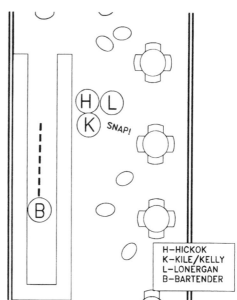

2. *9:16 pm: Kile places his Remington pistol against Bill's ear and pulls the trigger. It missfires. Bill manages to free his gun and fires a shot into Kile's wrist.*

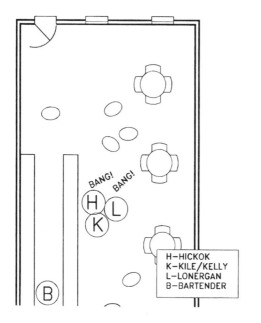

3. *9:17 pm: In the process of wrestling Lonergan, Bill fires a second shot into Kile's side, manages to shoot Lonergan in the knee, and gets free.*

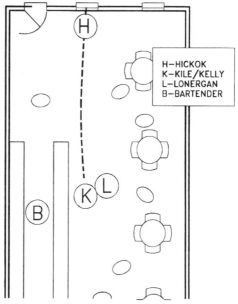

4. *9:18 pm: Hickok get's to his feet and sees himself surrounded by soldiers. Before they react, Bill charges to the rear of the saloon and dives through the window.*

Seventh Cavalry in 1870, who later retired as a captain) who intimated that the pair left Fort Hays "without permission" to visit Thomas Drum's saloon [sic], and thirty-nine years later in the Newton, Massachuetts, *Circuit* of September 3, 1909, he described what happened:

> Lonergan was a powerful man, and although he had been in the company only a short time he was considered one of the pugilists of M troop. When they arrived at the saloon Wild Bill . . . was standing at the bar having a sociable chat with the bar tender. Lonergan walked up behind Wild Bill without being discovered, and as quick as a flash he threw both arms around Wild Bill's neck, from the rear, and pulled him over backwards on to the floor, and held his arms out at full length. Lonergan and Wild Bill had had some words before that caused this action. In the meantime Wild Bill got his right hand free and slipped one of his pistols out of his holster. Some of the men in visiting this city were in the habit of carrying their pistols stuck down inside the waistband of their pants, with the hilt protruding, but covered up by their blouse, and a man could whip out one of those pistols in an instant. Kelly had his in this position, and he immediately whipped it out and put the muzzle into Wild Bill's ear, and snapped it. The pistol missed fire, or it would have ended his career then and there. Lonergan was holding Wild Bill's right wrist, but Bill turned his hand far enough to one side to enable him to fire his pistol, and the first shot went through the right wrist of Kelly. He fired a second time, and the bullet entered Kelly's side, went through his body, and could be felt on the other side. Of course Kelly was knocked out of service in a few seconds. Wild Bill did his best to kill Lonergan, who was holding him down, but Lonergan held his wrist in such a position that it was impossible for him to get a shot at his body. He finally fired again and shot Longergan through the knee cap. That caused Lonergan to release his hold on Wild Bill, who jumped up from the floor and made tracks for the back of the saloon, jumped through a window, taking the glass and sash with him, and made his escape. I was on the scene a few moments after Kelly breathed his last. A doctor was sent for. He asked me if Kelly was a friend of mine. I said that he was, and that both men were members of my company. He examined him thoroughly, and then removed a gold ring from Kelly's finger and handed it to me. I kept that ring for a few years, but I never could find any of Kelly's relations, though I tried diligently to do so. I was informed later that his name was Kyle,

Wild Bill fights fifteen angry Seventh Cavalry troopers as illustrated in Buel's **Heroes of the Plains.** *(Author's collection.)*

and that he belonged either in Chicago, Illinois, or Cincinatti, Ohio. Finally I gave this ring to a friend of mine, John Murphy, who was a trumpeter in my company and was wounded in the battle of the Wichita.

The news of this affair very quickly reached camp, and a number of the men seized their guns and started for Hayes [sic] City, where I joined the party, and we visited all the saloons and dives in the place, but we could not find Wild Bill. If we had found him we will leave it to the reader to imagine what would have happened to him. In the meantime, Kelly's body was taken to our camp and Lonergan was sent to the post hospital at Fort Hayes.

I saw Wild Bill about a year later, about 30 miles from Fort Harker, on the line of the Kansas Pacific railroad, either at the little town of Aberdeen [Abilene?] or Salina, Kansas, I have forgotten which, while going south in May 1871. Some of the officers and myself and a number of the men had a talk with him. He told us that after leaving Drum's saloon he went to the room that he occupied and took his Winchester rifle and 100 rounds of ammunition and proceeded to a cemetery [Boot Hill] a little west of the town. There he laid until daylight the next morning, as he expected the soldiers would round him

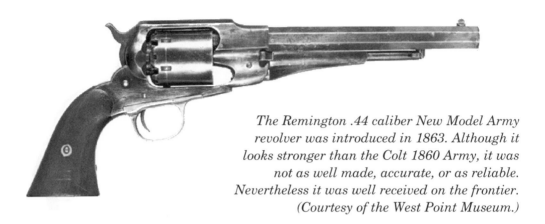

The Remington .44 caliber New Model Army revolver was introduced in 1863. Although it looks stronger than the Colt 1860 Army, it was not as well made, accurate, or as reliable. Nevertheless it was well received on the frontier. (Courtesy of the West Point Museum.)

up and end his career. He declared that he never intended to be taken alive in that cemetery, and would make many of those soldiers bite the dust before he would be taken. After daylight he left there and started for Big Creek station, on the line of the Kansas Pacific railroad, about eight miles east of this city, and boarded a train . . . Wild Bill told me once that he never ran up against a man that he was afraid of in a square pistol duel, but that he did expect sometime some desperado would come up and shoot him from the rear . . .

Ryan's memory betrayed him when he claimed that Kile died in the saloon. In fact, he was taken to the Post hospital and died on the 18th from wounds received "as a result of a drunken row and not in the line of duty." Curiously, having learned that "Kelly's real name was Kile, Ryan

continued to use the former name in his published account. Kile was given a military funeral and buried at Fort Hays, but some years later along with others buried there, his body was transferred to the military cemetery at Fort Leavenworth. As for Lonergan, he recovered and was returned to duty. Ironically, according to Ryan, Lonergan was killed later by a man named Kelly who belonged to an infantry regiment.

William E. Webb, one of the founders of Hays City, who knew Hickok well, mentioned the incident in his book *Buffalo Land,* published in 1872. He stated that "two soldiers attempted his life. Attacked unexpectedly, Bill was knocked down and the muzzle of a musket [*sic*] placed against his forehead, but before it could be discharged the ready pistol was drawn and the two soldiers fell down, one dead, the other badly

Tom Custer, brother of George Custer and winner of two Congressional Medals of Honor, was alleged by some writers to have led the troops seeking Hickok, but there is no evidence of this.

wounded. Their companions clamored for revenge, and Bill changed his base."[2]

By 1881, when most people, with the possible exception of the residents of Hays City, had all but forgotten the incident, James Buel, in his mammoth tome, *Heroes of the Plains,* recounted the story but upped the "ante" and Wild Bill was forced into a fight with fifteen troopers. He claimed that Hickok, acting in his capacity as city marshal, interceded when a number of drunken troopers invaded Paddy Welch's saloon on February 12, 1870 [*sic*], and was goaded into a fist fight with a sergeant, which rapidly degenerated into a gunfight between Hickok and fifteen troopers that left three troopers dead and Hickok wounded seven times!

There is no firm evidence of how many troopers might have been involved, but the question remains: was Wild Bill wounded in the fight? Ryan's account, the most detailed extant, makes no mention of Hickok being injured although several contemporary references to the shootout do suggest that Wild Bill was shot in the leg.

If this is true, who shot him? Lonergan was too busy, and Kile's pistol misfired. In reviewing the conflicting evidence, an expert on early

George Armstrong Custer, commanding officer of the 7th Cavalry. (Courtesy of the Library of Congress.)

Hays City history with access to all known records, expressed the opinion that if Buel was right and the initial fight did take place, then it is possible that when Kile saw his friend getting the worst of it, he attempted to murder Hickok but his pistol misfired; Hickok then managed to reach his own weapons and shot both Lonergan and Kile. He in turn was shot in the leg by one of their drunken companions. Regardless of how many there were, only a fool would attempt to fight it out with a crowd of drunken troopers.

Hickok's exit, therefore, was because he rightly decided that discretion was indeed the better part of valor when faced by such odds![3]

At this late date, we can only imagine the confused accounts that reached Fort Hays soon after the shooting. Indeed, Winfield S. Harvey, a blacksmith in Troop K, 7th Cavalry, writing in his diary on July 18, only hours after the shootout, named the soldiers as "Carrell and Flanigan." Claims made much later that a "dead or alive" order was issued for Wild Bill are not borne out by military records. And why should such an order be issued? Even General Custer accepted that shootouts between individuals were a common occurrence, and though he did not name him, he was referring to Kile when he remarked that one of Hickok's victims was "at that time a member of my command."

In fact, Lonergan and Kile, both understood to be drunk and technically "deserters," had attacked a civilian, and because their wounds were received "in a drunken row" and not in the line of duty, the military took no action.[4]

In this writer's opinion, perhaps the most interesting moment came when John Kile pushed the muzzle of his Remington pistol into Hickok's ear and it misfired. Luck was certainly on Hickok's side considering some companies of the Seventh Cavalry used the much vaunted (by today's shooters and collectors) .44 caliber Remington New Model Army pistol, which was first issued in 1863. Ordnance reports reveal that they were notorious for misfires or for blowing up on occasion.

For this, Wild Bill must have been eternally grateful![5]

Notes

1. Typed copy of an interview with Matt Clarkson by W. D. Philip, Manuscripts Division, Kansas State Historical Society (see also Rodney Staab, "The Matthew Clarkson Manuscripts," *Kansas History: A Journal of the Central Plains.* Winter, 1982, 256-278).

2. Webb, W. E. *Buffalo Land.* Cincinnati and Chicago, 1872, 146.

3. James W. Buel, *Heroes of the Plains.* New York and St. Louis, 1882, 117-124. James D. Drees to Joseph G. Rosa, June 14, 1999.

4. Typewritten copy of Harvey's diary in Container 6, the Edward S. Godfrey Papers, Manuscripts Division, Library of Congress.

5. Ordnance Records (1861-69), National Archives, Washington, D.C. (these records also contain 1867 correspondence from Fort Laramie concerning the poor performance of the Remington revolver— its tendency to blow up or misfire being the most crucial).

Chapter Eight

HICKOK AND HARDIN

Mention John Wesley Hardin to most Western buffs, and the conversation usually turns to his status as Texas's most famous "man-killer" (he claimed "forty notches") and his alleged confrontation with Wild Bill Hickok at Abilene, Kansas during June of 1871. In a near shootout, Hardin who had his eighteenth birthday about a week earlier, claims to have worked the "border roll" on Hickok and forced him to put up his pistols. Curiously, the alleged confrontation only came to light when his autobiography *The Life of John Wesley Hardin As Written by Himself* was published posthumously in 1896, one year after his death. Since then, some writers have cited Hardin's version verbatim with no attempt at verification, while others have gone to extraordinary lengths to debunk it, and the alleged showdown remains controversial.

It has also been claimed that Hardin adopted a shoulder holster when he discovered that Hickok had the edge over him when it came to "the draw." This is nonsense, of course, but in his book *Trigger-nometry,* Eugene Cunningham did report that Hardin was credited with designing a "holster vest" that was made of soft calf-skin (but he makes no mention of Wild Bill in this connection!). It contained two holster pockets which slanted the pistols so that they nestled beneath each arm, butts forward. All Wes had to do was to cross his arms and pull!

Hardin was a complex and volatile character; a man who sought notoriety and reacted violently when he thought he had been insulted. His best biographer, the late Richard Marohn, a psychiatrist, after a protracted examination of the Hickok-Hardin relationship, concluded that

John Wesley Hardin from a photograph said to have been made in Abilene in 1871. There was no photographer at Abilene at that time, so most of the cattlemen visited A. P. Trott's gallery at Junction City, who probably made this plate. (Courtesy Robert E. McNellis.)

Ben Thompson, the British-born gunfighter who was at odds with Wild Bill in Abilene. He is pictured here as Marshal of Austin, Texas. (Courtesy of the Rose Collection.)

Wes regarded Hickok as a "self object" and worshiped Wild Bill. Indeed, as early as 1888, writing to his wife from the Huntsville, Texas prison, he stated that "no braver man [than Hickok] ever drew breath." Dr. Marohn also disclosed that Hardin was a disturbed character who shed tears when frustrated and expressed a terror of being lynched. Yet this same character displayed an aggressive streak, which coupled with a talent with firearms, endeared him to some and aroused the hatred and contempt of others. And his reputation was not helped by his boastful accounts of his killings, which was a prominent feature of his book.[1] He also claimed that Ben Thompson, the British-born Texas gambler and gun-fighter, had tried to persuade him to confront Hickok because he always picked on "Southern men to kill." Wes retorted: "If Bill needs killing, why don't you kill him yourself?" "I would rather get someone else to do it," was Ben's reply.[2] One is left with the feeling that had Ben lived to read Wes's book he would have strenuously denied it. His record clearly shows that Ben was his own man and would not have relied upon others to fight his battles.

Here is how Wes described the alleged confrontation between himself and Hickok:

I spent most of my time in Abilene in the saloons and gambling houses, playing poker, faro, and seven-up.

John Wesley Hardin.
(Courtesy of the Rose
Collection.)

One day I was rolling ten pins and my best horse was hitched outside in front of the saloon. I had two six-shooters on, and, of course, I knew the saloon people would raise a row if I did not pull them off. Several Texans were there rolling ten pins and drinking. I suppose we were pretty noisy. Wild Bill came in and said we were making too much noise and told me to pull off my pistols until I got ready to go out of town. I told him I was ready to go now, but did not propose to put up my pistols, go or no go. He went out and I followed him. I started up the street when someone behind me shouted out, "Set up. All down but nine."

Wild Bill whirled around and met me. He said, "What are you howling about, and what are you doing with those pistols on?"

I said, "I am just taking in the town."

He pulled his pistol and said, "Take those pistols off. I arrest you."

I said all right and pulled them out of the scabbard[s], but while he was reaching for them, I reversed them and whirled them over on him with the muzzles in his face, springing back at the same time. I told him to put his pistols up, which he did. I cursed him for a long-haired scoundrel that would shoot a boy with his back to him (as I had been told he intended to do me). He said, "Little Arkansaw, you have been wrongly informed."

I shouted, "This is my fight and I'll

THE BORDER ROLL

The technique that Hardin supposedly used when Hickok was attempting to arrest him.

1. The hands are held well away from the pistol butts.

2. When requested to hand over his weapons, the gunfighter eases them out of the holsters.

3. As they come forward, they begin to turn so that the butts face up.

4. They start to swing forward and the butts turn toward the hands.

5. The revolvers are leveled and held in position, ready for firing.

1. Hickok asks Hardin for his guns.

THE BORDER ROLL

A demonstration showing how Hardin may have gotten the drop on Wild Bill. (Vince Bergdale as Hickok and Jake Hopkins as Hardin.)

2. Hardin eases his guns out of their holsters

3. As they come forward, Hardin begins to turn them so the butts face up.

4. Hardin swings his guns forward and the butts turn toward the hands.

5. The swing is complete, the pistols are now cocked and ready for use.

Manning Clements, a cousin of Hardin, and one of the trouble-makers in Abilene. (Courtesy of the Rose Collection.)

Before we examine that statement further, it is important that we consider the fact that the alleged confrontation lacks any contemporary backing. Wild Bill, a Northerner, was not popular with some of the Texans, who would have welcomed Hardin's trick, and word of it would soon have found its way back to Texas. This is especially important when we consider a report published in the Kansas City *Journal of Commerce* of August 13, 1871, which alleged that Hickok had a "spite" against a Texas drover and hit him over the head with his revolver. He then "stamped him in the face with his boot heel, inflicting a severe wound." Other Texans present then told Wild Bill he would not be safe over night. He ignored them, which prompted the reporter to add that they "mistook their man, as 'Wild Bill' is the last man to be driven away by such threats. At last accounts he was still there and unharmed. Such a marshal might do for such a place as Abilene, but for Kansas City we don't want him."

Some might think that incident (which escaped the pages of the *Chronicle* and, apparently, the rest of the Kansas press) would have been seen by Hardin as an attack on "Texas boys" that needed some kind of retribution. But it is doubtful that he heard of it, for he had other things on his mind.

On July 5, one of Hardin's friends,

kill the first man that fires a gun."

Bill said, "You are the gamest and quickest boy I ever saw. Let us compromise this matter and I will be your friend. Let us go in here and take a drink, as I want to talk to you and give you some advice."

At first I thought he might be trying to get the drop on me, but he finally convinced me of his good intentions, and we went in and took a drink. We went into a private room and I had a long talk with him and we came out friends.

Abilene, Kansas as it appeared about at the time Hickok was City Marshal. (Courtesy of Kansas State Historical Society.)

William Cohron, a fellow Texan who had accompanied Wes up the trail from Texas, was murdered by a Mexican, Juan Bideno. Cohron's friends, according to Wes, urged him to track Bideno down since they had been unsuccessful in finding him.

Wes claimed that he was appointed a deputy sheriff and given letters of authority to present to any cattlemen that he met during his search, but there is no evidence of any such appointment. In reporting Cohron's murder in its issue of July 13, 1871, the Abilene *Chronicle* reported that Bideno had murdered Cohron because Cohron had ordered him to join another herd; and, taking "umbrage at the order," he waited for his chance and shot Cohron in the back.

Hardin, accompanied by two other Texans set off in pursuit on the morning of the July 6 and were later joined by John Cohron, the dead man's brother. They found Bideno in Summer City having lunch in the Southwestern Hotel.

The Oxford, Kansas *Times* of July 13, 1871, described how the unnamed Mexican was shot between the eyes as he sat drinking coffee, the shot "passing through the head and the partition, barely missing a lady in the next room, and was flattened against the stove." The editor also noted that the Mexican's "fine horse" was taken by his killer which he asserted was the property of the murdered Texan, adding that since the Mexican was dead, "he could not give his side of the story."

On August 6, Wes was again the center of attention when he murdered fellow Texan Charles Couger

John Wesley Hardin jumps from his hotel window after shooting a man to escape the wrath of Marshal Hickok who would be coming to arrest him. (Courtesy of The Authentic Life of John Wesley Hardin.)

at the American House. Couger, according to the Abilene *Chronicle* of August 10, was a "boss cattle herder" who was sitting on his bed reading a newspaper when four shots were fired at him through the wall by "Arkansaw Clemens" (the name Hardin was apparently known by in town), one of which pierced his heart killing him instantly. Fearful of what Hickok might do, Hardin skipped town. The *Chronicle* added that: "The murderer escaped and has thus far eluded his pursuers. If caught he will probably be killed on sight." Some writers, including his best biographer, have concluded that perhaps Hardin was not the murderer, but it was his cousin Wesley Clements (apparently they swapped names when it suited them). However, the Abilene *Chronicle* on August 17, in reporting the arrival of Cohron's tombstone, added that the man who killed Bideno also "killed Charles Couger on the 6th inst., in this place."

Hardin's description of how he worked the "border roll" on Hickok, reveals several discrepancies. His claim that Hickok "pulled his pistol" would have left him with one hand free. But when Wes pulled his own pistols and thrust the "muzzles in his [Hickok's] face," he then ordered Hickok to "put his pistols up, which he did." This was either sloppy writing by Hardin or errors by the typesetter or proof reader. The point be-

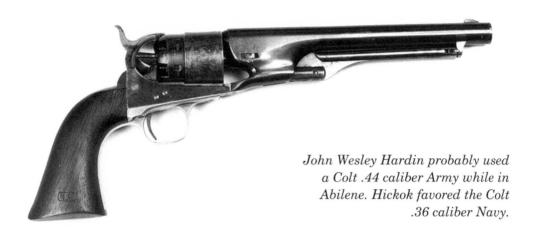

John Wesley Hardin probably used a Colt .44 caliber Army while in Abilene. Hickok favored the Colt .36 caliber Navy.

ing that when anyone pulls a pistol in a confrontation situation, it is either cocked and fired in one movement or held cocked, and ready for use. It should also be remembered that when ordered to disarm, it was usual to unbuckled the gunbelt, drop it and step aside without touching the pistols. Hardin could easily have pulled that trick on individuals unused to firearms, but Hickok had been around long enough to be aware of the "border roll" and similar tricks. As for later "recollections" by Hardin's relatives and others who claimed to have witnessed the event, one suspects that they, too, were influenced more by his autobiography than by personal involvement.

Another facet of the alleged confrontation concerns the pistols used by both parties, and how they were carried. Where Hickok favored the Colt's Model 1851 Navy pistol, Wes was reputed to favor the .44 Colt's

Army model of 1860. Yet his biographer reproduces a photograph of him sporting a Navy model, which in all probability was the type of weapon he carried in Abilene. We know that Hickok wore his pistols holstered butts forward in the customary manner of the time.

So it is also likely that Hardin followed his example. If so, and we accept his claim that he removed both pistols from their holsters, it would be a simple matter to place a hand under the butt of each pistol, ease them forward and slip his index fingers into the guards as he extended both pistols butts forward. As Hickok reached for them, he could step back, and spin or "roll" the muzzles, and lock his thumbs over the hammers to cock the pistols as the barrels came level, dead on target.

Hickok, of course, would have been watching him very carefully. Remember also that he had cocked

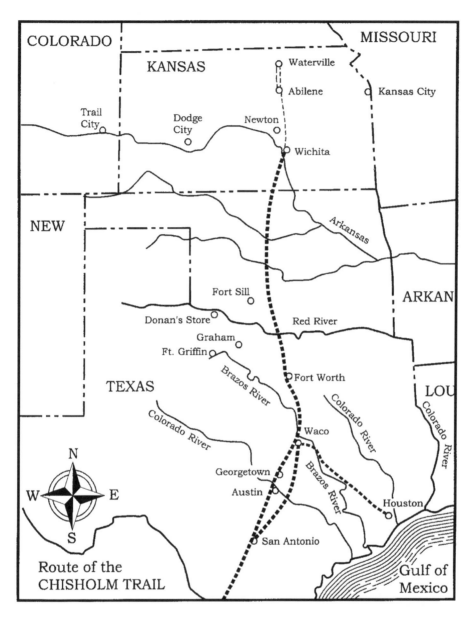

The Chisholm Trail ran up from Texas, crossed several rivers, went through
Indian Territory, and ended at Wichita. The route to Texas was established from
his home by Jesse Chisholm, a part Indian trader who lived among the Wichita
Indians. From Wichita northward to Abilene, the trail became "McCoy's Extension" or "The Abilene Trail." Here it met the tracks of the Union Pacific Railway
(Eastern Division) that became the Kansas Pacific Railway in 1869. Then a short
extension from Abilene to Waterville where it met the tracks of the Union Pacific
Railroad, Central Branch was added. Later, other trails up from Texas were
established that put Newton, Wichita, Caldwell, and Dodge City on the map; but
the Chisholm Trail is best remembered.

pistols lined up on Hardin, and in order to reach for Hardin's pistols, offered butts forward, Hickok would have to uncock and holster his own pistols. Hardin, in his autobiography hinted that Hickok was no fool and admitted that he had a "fine sense and was a splendid judge of human nature." In 1874, an anonymous writer had noted that Wild Bill was "cunning, and we may on good authority add that he is tricky."

So here we have Hardin himself and another crediting Hickok with a street-wise reaction to people and confrontations, which makes one wonder why such an individual should place any trust in a loud-mouthed eighteen year-old youth who had murdered five Mexican herders en route to Abilene, and then revenged himself upon another who was alleged to have murdered his friend Billy Cohron. Not surprisingly, we are left with the feeling that Hardin's claim was more wish fulfillment than fact.[3]

Dr. Marohn, in conversation with this writer, said that he had found no contemporary support for the alleged showdown with Hickok, and suggested that perhaps Hardin's admiration for Wild Bill prompted him to include Hickok as one of his "border roll" victims, for by 1895 Hardin's ego was badly in need of a boost. His latest biographer, however,

remains convinced that it must have happened simply because "there is no evidence that Hardin lied," which in itself raises the question of proof![4]

Prior to his capture by the Texas Rangers in 1877, Wes was reported to have practiced his expertise with a six-shooter on a large number of individuals, few of whom were his equal but became his victims. Therefore, it is only conjecture to assume what might have happened had Hardin and Hickok really opened fire upon each other face-to-face.

Notes

1. Richard C. Marohn, *The Last Gunfighter: John Wesley Hardin* (College Station, Texas, 1995), 312. A copy of Hardin's letter to his wife was kindly provided the writer by Chuck Parsons.

2. Hardin, *The Life of John Wesley Hardin (Sequin, Texas, 1896)*, 44.

3. *Ibid.*, 56; West Chester (Pennsylvania) *Daily Local News*, August 11, 1873.

4. Leon Metz, *John Wesley Hardin: Dark Angel of Texas* (Norman, Oklahoma, 1998), 53.

Chapter Nine

ABILENE: THE PHIL COE SHOOTOUT

Abilene is a name to conjure with: named after the Biblical city of the plains, it has been featured in innumerable books and movies. As the first of the Kansas cowtowns, it set the scene for those that succeeded it. It was built either side of the railroad tracks, (north was the respectable side while the south housed most of the gambling halls and houses of prostitution), and during the cattle season (May to October) it was a hive of activity. Down at the loading pens, Texas longhorn cattle were watered and fed prior to being loaded into the freight cars. Many suffered the further indignity of being dehorned to save themselves and other animals from injury during transit.

This cacophony of bawling bovines, the shrill shrieks of locomotive whistles and the crash of shunting cars, was accompanied by an all pervading cloud of dust and the stench of cattle. During the day, the town was quiet, but at night the image of Abilene was one of kerosene street lamps flickering in the darkness, garishly lit saloons, gambling halls and bawdy houses. Normal street noise was boosted by the muted strains of violins and banjos, or the strident sound of trumpets accompanied by the rhythmic thumping of pianos in or out of tune. All this to the sound of laughter, shouts, the clink of glasses or poker chips and the mad stamping of cowboys dancing. And in the early days, the sudden roar of a six-shooter was common.

Hickok's brief but hectic period as the Marshal of Abilene is perhaps better known today than his exploits at Springfield, Missouri, or Hays City. This is probably due to Hollywood movies and the attention cow (or cattle) towns have received at the hands of historians and novelists. For the lure of a town besieged by half-

Loading longhorn cattle could be dangerous. Sometimes the horns had a spread of seven feet which necessitated sawing them off to protect other animals and their handlers. (Author's collection.)

wild longhorn cattle and "unreconstructed" Texans anxious to refight the Civil War, and held at bay by one man, is a dominant theme in many a "Western" movie or novel. The fact that there were times when noted individuals, aided by several deputies, were all that stood between anarchy and law and order, is potent stuff, and explains why Hickok has been vested with the mantle of "town tamer" or "civilizer" by some writers who pointedly ignore his "hired help."

But all that was in the future early in 1867. At that time Abilene was a small halt on the tracks of the Union Pacific Railway Company (Eastern Division). Originally a stagecoach stop, it was still only a hamlet when Joseph G. McCoy, a cattle buyer from Illinois, arrived. He was anxious to find a point from which to ship Texas cattle to Eastern markets, and one that would not contravene state legislation against the longhorn cattle. The animals carried a tic that transferred splenic fever (commonly called Texas fever) to domestic stock. Prior to the Civil War, and quarantine laws, Texans had driven their cattle up to such diverse places as Sedalia, Missouri.,

Chicago, Illinois., and as far away as New York or California. During the war, when trail-driving stopped, Texas cattle had run wild and multiplied, so there was an urgent need for markets to boost the state's economy.

One obvious route north was a trail made by Jesse Chisholm a half-Indian trader who had plied between Texas and the Wichita Indians in Kansas. His trail went straight north up through what was then termed "Indian Territory" (present day Oklahoma) and encompassed the Canadian and the Arkansas rivers. This well watered and well provisioned route was ideal for the purpose. The snag, of course, was resistance to the longhorns and their tics by the farmers and homesteaders en route. In 1867, Kansas had a rethink on the quarantine laws, and it was agreed that provided the cattle were driven through uninhabited areas so as to avoid contact with domestic stock, they could enter the state. McCoy seized his chance and, following a lot of hard bargaining, the residents of Abilene finally agreed to sell McCoy land on which to build shipping pens, and he also reached an agreement with the U.P.E.D. who would pay him $5 for each carload of cattle shipped.

Within weeks the shipping pens were erected and the railroad had built a switch to handle one hundred cattle cars. On September 5, 1867, the first of many trains loaded with Texas cattle set out for the East. The Texans had driven them north over Chisholm's trail to where it ended at Wichita. From there "McCoy's Extension" or "The Abilene Trail" carried it on to Abilene. And for four years Abilene enjoyed a good living from the trade as well as suffering its drawbacks—the influx of gamblers, pimps, prostitutes and others anxious to relieve the Texans of their hard-earned wages.

The Texas longhorns were driven up the trail by a mixture of the races. Although the majority of the cowboys were white (blacks became more prominent in the 1870s), there were a large number of Mexican vaqueros on the trail in the late 1860s and early 1870s. Despite being indebted to them for much of their cowboy technique (which in turn owed its origins to Spain), feeling against Mexicans among the Texans ran high—they still remembered "The Alamo."

John Wesley Hardin shot several of them on the trail to Abilene late in April 1871. But the Texans' anger was directed not only against Mexicans and some blacks, but against each other. Feuds and personal disputes were bottled up on the trail, but once they were free to roam the

The Drover's Cottage sits near the tracks as loaded cattle cars trundle past. (Author's collection.)

streets of a cowtown, Texan against Texan fights broke out. Many people and some of the Kansas press described the cowboys as those "murderous Texans," and some of them did their best to live up to their reputation. Perhaps the worst incident involving feuding Texans occurred at Newton on August 20, 1871, when in reprisal for the killing of one of their own by an Ohioan, a number of them ambushed him in a saloon. During the ensuing gunfight, several men were killed and others wounded in what is remembered as "Newton's General Massacre." In its report of the fight, *The Kansas Daily Common-wealth* of August 21 described the affair as worse than "Tim Finnegan's wake."

But many Texans shared the townsfolks' abhorrence of such behavior, and did their best to avoid feuds and to forget the war and concentrate upon economic links with Northern markets. Nevertheless, it was the actions of the troublemakers that placed the police on their guard.

From 1867 until May 1870 Abilene had no established law and order and relied upon local township constables. But the appointment of Tom Smith as its first Marshal or

Joseph G. McCoy, the first elected mayor of Abilene and "father" of the cattle trade. (Author's collection.)

Chief of Police following its incorporation as a third-class city, soon changed attitudes. Smith proved highly popular and efficient, but his murder in November 1870 at the hands of two settlers left the city in need of a new marshal. Several people were employed as stopgap policemen, but it was the appointment of Wild Bill on April 15, 1871, that finally convinced the Texans that as with Smith, they could no longer dictate terms. Wild Bill, although respected by the Texans as a fighting man, was nevertheless disliked because he represented the "Northerners" or "Yanks" against whom most of them had fought in the Civil War.

Hickok's rule in Abilene lasted eight months, during which time he kept the peace aided by several deputies. His methods have met with criticism, mostly from people of a later time who did not appreciate the situation. Some of his contemporaries, however, thought him overbearing and too fond of gambling, while others accepting his passions nonetheless appreciated the effect his presence had upon the lawless element. As for the citizens of Abilene, few of them knew him as a person; but shared his distrust of the Texans. Nonetheless, they tolerated them because of the effect that they had upon the city's economy.

McCoy's Great Western Stockyard, one small part of the shipping pens and system of gates to control the number of cattle handled at one time. (Courtesy of Kansas State Historical Society.)

Consequently, Hickok's shootout with Phil Coe on October 5, 1871, which ended with the tragic death of a friend and erstwhile city jailer, left its mark both upon Hickok and Abilene's already strained relationship with the cattle trade.

By early October, with the end of the cattle season, many of the drovers faced financial losses. According to the Lawrence *Republican Journal* of October 19, 1871, those who had held cattle at Abilene in expectation of higher prices were forced to sell them short or winter them. An added problem was the shortage of freight cars and low prices offered at Kansas City, which left many of the Texans feeling disgruntled. Despite this situation, a number of cowboys and drovers had remained behind to visit the Dickinson County Fair. In fact, there was really little else for them to do since the city council in September had ordered Marshal Hickok to close down most of the brothels and gambling dens. Not surprisingly, the events surrounding the shootout between Hickok and Coe are fraught with contradiction. Legend asserts

Some of the cattle cars at Abilene. (Author's collection.)

that the pair had recently come to blows over the favors of a prostitute. Others (including some press reports) hinted at an undisclosed dispute between the pair and Coe's reported vow to get Hickok "before the frost." On the evening of October 5, however, Abilene was seething with Texans bemoaning the heavy rain which had dampened their enthusiasm for the fair. Some prepared to return home, while others sought solace in whiskey and by early evening many of them, drunk and belligerent, began touring the saloons on Texas Street, forcing people to accept or buy drinks.

At about 9 p.m. according to the *Chronicle* on October 14, some time after Hickok had warned the Texans against carrying firearms within city limits, a shot was fired close to the Alamo Saloon. Hickok soon appeared and demanded to know who fired it. He was confronted by Phil Coe, pistol in hand, backed by about fifty armed Texans. Coe said that he had shot at a stray dog. He then pulled a second pistol and fired twice at Wild Bill. One shot hit the ground between Hickok's legs and the other zipped through the tail of his coat. Wild Bill's reaction, as he drew his own two pistols, was as "as quick as thought" according to the editor of the *Chronicle*. He shot Coe twice in the stomach and

Theodore C. Henry, the first acting mayor of Abilene who hired Tom Smith. In later years Henry became incolved in wheat growing. (Courtesy the Kansas State Historical Society.)

fired at another man who ran between them pistol in hand. The *Chronicle* also stated that "others in the crowd were hurt," which suggests that either Coe or Hickok fired more shots. Or perhaps Coe's shot passed through Hickok's coat and then hit someone in the crowd. Far more likely, some of the Texans may also have opened fire.

Less than a month before his death on March 9, 1932, aged 80, William B. Smith, who was in Abilene at the time of the shooting, stated that one of the Texans was shot in the arm and taken to the Bull's Head Saloon where he was laid on a gaming table while his arm was attended to. Coe was carried to his rooms on Cedar street which he shared with an unnamed woman. The doctors discovered that his wounds were mortal, and he died three days later in great agony. Smith also recalled placing a stove in Coe's bedroom the next day.[1]

When Hickok discovered that the other man he had shot was his friend Mike Williams, he carried him into the Alamo and laid him gently down on a billiard table. It was reported that tears ran down his face as he turned and stalked out of the place demanding that every man disarm, and hustling and shoving aside any Texans who were foolish enough

This woodcut graphically shows how Texans dressed and carried their pistols during the early days in Abilene. (Author's collection.)

to get in his way. Within an hour they had all gone.

In more than a century since that shootout, all manner of allegations have been made concerning what happened. We have summarized events based upon the benefit of hindsight and research, but a review of some contemporary reactions and misinformation may also be appreciated. On October 7, the Leavenworth *Commercial* ran a piece describing the shooting and the accidental killing of Williams; but on the 8th, citing the report of the Kansas City *Times* (based on the word of a Kansas Pacific Railway brakeman), it was stated that Hickok "shot two of his police force and killed them, while engaged in a dispute with them. They fired the first shot and missed the Marshal, when he drew and

placed both *hors du combat*. One of the men killed is said to be Mike Williams, formerly proprietor of the Walnut Exchange, corner of Twelfth and Main streets in this city."

On October 12, the Atchison *Daily Champion,* cited the Lawrence *Journal's* version which alleged that a colored man "who came down on the train from Abilene," reported that Williams and another man had been drinking and becoming intoxicated attacked Wild Bill. Williams fired at Hickok but missed. "Bill immediately drew and fired twice at him, both shots taking effect in the body killing him instantly. He then turned and shot the other, whose name was Philip Cole, a Texan, through the stomach, and it was thought he could not live until morning."

The Warrensburg, Missouri,

Philip Coe, the Texas gambler who shot it out with Wild Bill and lost. (Courtesy Chuck Parsons.)

Thomas James "Bear River Tom" Smith, was Marshal of Abilene from May until November 1870 when he was murdered. Tom was greatly admired. (Courtesy the Kansas State Historical Society.)

Standard on October 12, also intimated that Hickok had "murdered" two of his policemen. But on the 19th, it reprinted the Kansas City *Times* report (copied from the Abilene *Chronicle*) which set the record straight and relieved a number of Hickok's friends who lived in the city. Fortunately, most of the other papers were closer to the facts.

The Junction City *Union* on the 7th in reviewing the events that led up to the shooting and Coe's avowed declaration to get Hickok "before the frost," went on:

As a reply to the Marshal's demand that order should be preserved, some of the party fired upon him, when drawing his pistols he "fired with marvelous rapidity and characteristic accuracy," as our informant expressed it, shooting a Texan named Coe, the keeper of the saloon, we believe, through the abdomen, and grazing one or two more.

In the midst of the firing, a policeman rushed in to assist Bill, but unfortunately got in the line of fire. It being dark, Bill did not recognize him, and supposed him to be one of

The Phil Coe Gunfight

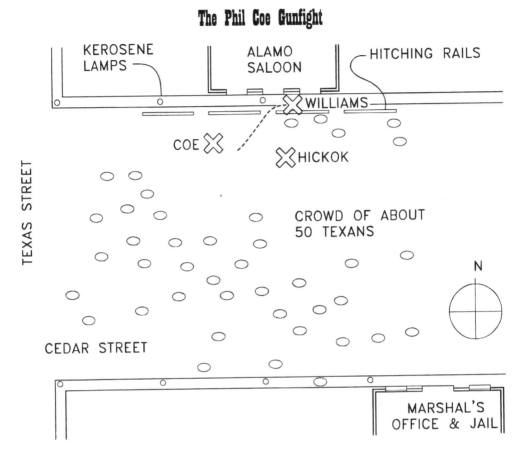

The positions of Hickok, Phil Coe, and Mike Williams in front of the Alamo Saloon are shown here. This sketch is based upon a careful examination of available evidence and eyewitness reports. Williams, Hickok's friend, is believed to have hurried out of the Alamo and run between Hickok and Coe. Having just shot it out with Coe, Wild Bill then fired at the unrecognized man. In the flickering glare of kerosene street lamps and the milling, drunken mob, Hickok only saw him as a fast-moving man with a pistol in hand who was a threat.

the party. He was instantly killed. Bill greatly regrets the shooting of his friend. Coe will die. The verdict of the citizens seemed to be unanimously in support of the Marshal, who bravely did his duty.

The Burlingame *Weekly Osage Chronicle* of October 12 (as did some other papers) made a point of discussing the poor state of the weather and the effect the rain had upon the Texans. It also injected a macabre note presumably in an attempt at humor.

The Phil Coe Gunfight
October 5, 1871
Abilene, Kansas

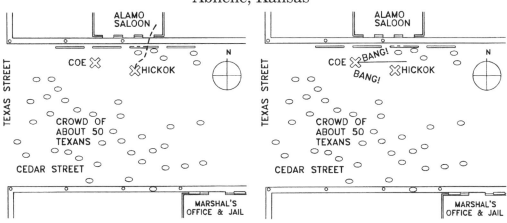

1. October 5, 1871, 9:00 pm: After warning the Texans to not carry guns, Hickok hears a gunshot from the direction of the Alamo Saloon run by Phil Coe. Hickok meets Coe in the street and asks who fired the shot. Coe, with gun in hand, says that he shot at a dog.

2. 9:01 pm: Without warning, Coe fires two shots at Hickok; both miss. Bill draws both his Colt Navies and shoots Phil Coe in the upper body. Mike Williams hears the shots being fired in the street that is dimly lit by kerosene street lamps.

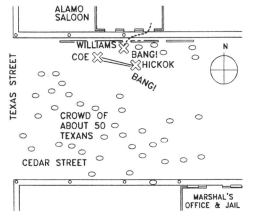

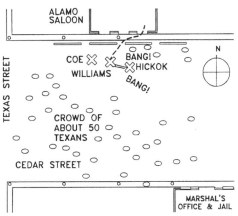

3. 9:02 pm: As Coe falls to the ground, Williams runs in the direction of the shot and between Hickok and Coe.

2. 9:02 pm: Hickok instinctly fires at the shadowy figure that has moved into his line of fire, thinking he is one of the Texans. Williams falls fatally wounded.

The Texans it was alleged amused themselves by "taking men by force from their places of business and compelling them to treat. Considerable scuffling in doing this resulted in much noise and excitement.

At last the City Marshal, Wild Bill, was attempting to quell the riot and disperse the squad, when one of them, Paul Cole [sic], an Austin, Texas, gambler, let loose his pistol, but hit no one. Bill drew his weapon and winged Cole, shooting him through the arm, but unfortunately the bullet from Bill's piece, seeming to realize that, coming from Bill's hand, its mission would not be fully performed without taking a life, passed through the heart of Mike Williams killing him almost instantly." Noting that Mike's wife had advised him that she was sick and needed him, and he was preparing to take the Denver express home, it declared: "When the train left Abilene at 9:45 Bill and others were on the trail of Phil Cole and more bloodshed was anticipated."

The Wyandotte *Gazette* of October 12, (citing the Lawrence *Journal*) also agreed with the Abilene *Chronicle* that Hickok and Coe were only about eight feet apart when they exchanged shots. Wild Bill, though shot at four times, "escaped unhurt." It then noted that after the affray he went through the town and "dis-

armed all persons wearing pistols. The Texans fled to their holes and were not to be found the next morning."

Perhaps the most interesting and inaccurate account appeared in the Oxford, Kansas, *Times*, of October 21. Its inconsistency might be accounted for by the text being "pied up" (a printers' expression for errors and omissions). Coe is described at one point as Philip H. Wilson who was protecting a young man named "Harding" who was quite drunk. Fearing a possible accident, Coe/Wilson took his revolver from him. Coe then used it to shoot at a dog. The report then goes on:

[Wild] Bill went to the door [of the Alamo saloon] and asked who fired it, when Coe said he had fired it at a dog. Bill asked him what he was doing with the pistol in his hand, but before Coe could answer, a friend to one side called to him and while his head was turned, Bill drew a pistol and fired. Coe instantly fired three shots at the Marshal from the pistol he had in his hand, but the latter dodged behind a door and escaped. Coe then fell into the arms of his friends. With a revolver in each hand, Bill then started to run down the stairs from the saloon which is in the second story [sic], and meeting Mike Williams at the bottom fired a shot from each revolver, both balls passing through his body. It is said that the above are the facts in the case, and that there was no other provocation for the shooting. Coe is said to have been a kind and generous hearted man well thought of by all who knew him. He had many friends among the Texans and cattle dealers about Abilene. It is darkly hinted that avengers are on the trail and we will probably soon hear of another tragedy in Abilene.

Coe's character has long been the subject of controversy among Texans and Kansans. Theophilus Little recalled him as a "red mouthed, bawling 'thug-'plug' Ugly-a very dangerous beast." Some fellow Texans naturally sided with him against Northerners, while others who knew him well recalled that despite his great height (6 feet 4 inches and weighing over 200 pounds) during the late war he had avoided combat by deserting from the Confederate army or getting himself hospitalized when suffering from gonorrhea. Therefore, his threat to get Hickok "before the frost" seems out of character. Nevertheless, the Texas press supported its dead son. The Austin *Weekly State Journal* of October 26 summed up popular feeling and declared that the "gallows and penitentiary are the places to tame such blood thirsty wretches as 'Wild Bill.'"[2]

Coe's body was returned to Texas, but enroute his unembalmed corpse forced a hasty burial at Brenham. Wild Bill, meanwhile, arranged for the shipment of Mike Williams's body back to Kansas City. He also paid the funeral expenses; but there was no mention of him attending when Williams was buried with all the pomp the McGee Hook and Ladder Company could muster. The procession to the burial ground on Jefferson street between Eleventh and Twelfth streets was accompanied by a band.[3] In its coverage of the funeral, the Kansas City *Journal of Commerce* on October 8 agreed that the shooting "was purely accidental." It went on to describe the terrible shock Mike's death had been for his young 19-year-old wife. "She bears her sorrow now, calmly, yet it will never be forgotten." Some time later when he visited Kansas City (he was there late in December 1871), Wild Bill himself is reported to have explained to her what happened, and expressed his deep regret.

Any suggestion that Hickok ambushed Coe is not corroborated by the contemporary Kansas press. The fact that they were only about eight feet apart and facing each other when they opened fire, suggests that Coe was either a poor shot or drunk. The coroner's inquest held next day exonerated Hickok. Unfortunately, it is

Philip H. Coe, Jr. is buried in the Prairie Lea Cemetery of Brenham, Texas in range 2, lot 2.

understood to have perished along with other historic documents in a courthouse fire in 1879, otherwise we would have access to witnesses' statements.

According to Charles Gross, soon after the Coe fight, Hickok began carrying a sawed-off shotgun on a strap under his coat.[4]

Late in November, Hickok took the train to Topeka for a rest from his duties in Abilene. According to the Topeka *Daily Commonwealth* of November 25, Hickok had been advised several times that there was a price on his head, and some days before a letter had been received stating that "a purse of $11,000 had been made up and five men were on their way to Abilene" to kill him.

They kept hidden, but when he noticed "four desperate looking fellows headed by a desperado about six feet four inches high" and heard the big man say: "Wild Bill is going on the train," he was immediately on his guard. Their attempts to get behind him were frustrated and they headed for the forward car, while Hickok remained in the rear. While a friend kept watch he slept, but when the five men appeared in the car, and the leader positioned himself behind him, pistol in hand, Hickok was woken up. The train was about ten miles out of Topeka when he made his move. As the train pulled into the depot, he was able to see his friend safely onto a bus and return to the car just as the Texans tried to leave.

Hickok faced them down and demanded to know where they were going. "We propose to stop in Topeka," was the response. "I am satisfied that you are hounding me," retorted Wild Bill, "and as I intend to stop in Topeka, you can't stop here."

They immediately objected, but "a pair of 'em convinced the murderous Texans that they had better go on which they did. While we cannot justify lawlessness or recklessness of any kind, yet we think the marshal wholly justifiable in his conduct toward such a party. Furthermore, we think he is entitled to the thanks of the law-abiding citizens throughout the State for the safety of life and property at Abilene, which has been secured, more through his daring, than any other agency."[5]

On January 11, 1872, three months after Coe's death, the editor of the *Chronicle* reflected popular opinion when he compared Coe's demise with that of the notorious Jim Fisk who was killed by the jealous lover of Fisk's mistress. Fisk's murder in New York caused an uproar, but "when the gambler Phil Cole [*sic*] was shot in Abilene, nearly everybody said 'served him right.'"

Whatever the rights or wrongs of Hickok's fight with Phil Coe, it is an undeniable fact that its outcome served to further the already growing part-fact part-mythical reputation of Wild Bill Hickok as the West's premier gunfighter and a "terror to evildoers."

Notes

1. Statement by William B. Smith before H. L. Humphry in February, 1932. The Kansas Collection, University of Kansas Library, Lawrence, Kansas.

2. Theophilus Little, "Early Days of Abilene and Dickinson County," Adolph Roenigk (editor) *Pioneer History of Kansas*, Lincoln, Kansas, 1933, 37-38.

3. The cemetery was closed to burials in 1876. In 1872 the Catholic church purchased a new site for burials south of town, the first burial taking place in 1873. Most of the bodies from the original cemetery were moved to the new one in 1882 when Kansas City expanded. However an exhaustive search of available records has failed to disclose any mention of Michael Williams (Father Michael Coleman, Diocese of Kansas City, St. Joseph, to Joseph G. Rosa, Febrary 12, 27 and March 16, 2000).

4. Charles Gross to J. B. Edwards, June 15, 1925 (Manuscripts Division, Kansas State Historical Society, Topeka, Kansas).

5. This article headed "Attempt to Kill Marshal Hickok," was published verbatim without comment by the Abilene *Chronicle* on November 30, 1871. It is not generally known that the story appeared originally in the *Commonwealth*.

Chapter Ten

ACES AND EIGHTS

General George A. Custer's 1874 Expedition confirmed what some people already knew—that there was gold in the Black Hills—but few would have guessed what an impact it would have upon the region. Although set aside by treaty as a Sioux reservation in 1868, neither legislation nor troops were able to deter would be goldseekers, and by the time Hickok reached the region early in 1876, camps or embryo townships had sprung up, but one in particular was to achieve immortality—Deadwood.

It lay in a natural gulch that ended against a canyon wall. Laid out on April 28, 1876, within weeks it boasted a main street that meandered between tree stumps, boulders and potholes; but by June strewn along its length were a number of rough-hewn wooden shack-like buildings and some sidewalks. Soon this area of unsurpassed beauty, with its dense trees creating the appearance of "black hills," streams and fresh, clean air, was polluted by campfire smoke and the landscape scarred by the labors of hundreds of people as they erected tents or shacks. More permanent structures had been erected by July, and main street was now the site of saloons, stores, and a theater, catering for all tastes,day and night. By the time Hickok arrived, Deadwood was thriving.

Following his marriage to Agnes Lake on March 5, 1876, Wild Bill returned west to prepare an expedition to the Black Hills. Hints in the St. Louis press, where he spent some time early in the year, suggest that he had already visited the region and was now anxious to return. Indeed, it is possible that he ventured into the Hills as early as 1875, but that has yet to be confirmed. However,

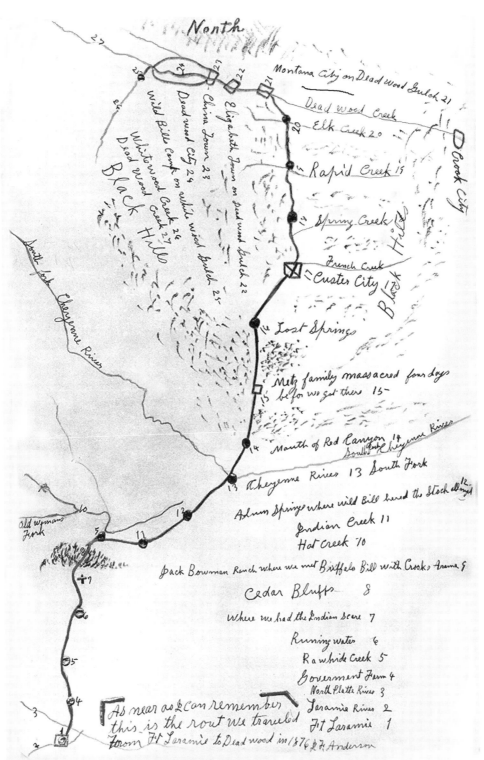

*White Eye Anderson's sketch of the route from Cheyenne to Deadwood.
(Courtesy of the late Raymond W. Thorp.)*

A mountain-top view of Deadwood's mainstreet overlooking the area where Hickok was killed. (Author's collection.)

according to the Cheyenne *Daily Sun* of April 30, Hickok had dispatched circulars and posters to many of the leading papers in the region announcing that he was organizing an expedition which would leave on May 17. Each man was to arm himself with a good rifle, 200 rounds of ammunition, one tent for two or more persons, a rubber blanket, woolen blankets and four to six months' provisions. As it turned out, Hickok's expedition was cancelled; some believe because most of those who would have accompanied him joined up with C. C. Carpenter's outfit instead which was to leave earlier. In any event, by June of 1876 Hickok was back in Cheyenne where he joined forces with Charles Utter, better known as "Colorado Charlie" and his brother Steve. The three are believed to have known each other for some years, so it was a fortuitous meeting insofar as Wild Bill was concerned. The trip would also give Charlie a chance to complete plans for his proposed pony express service

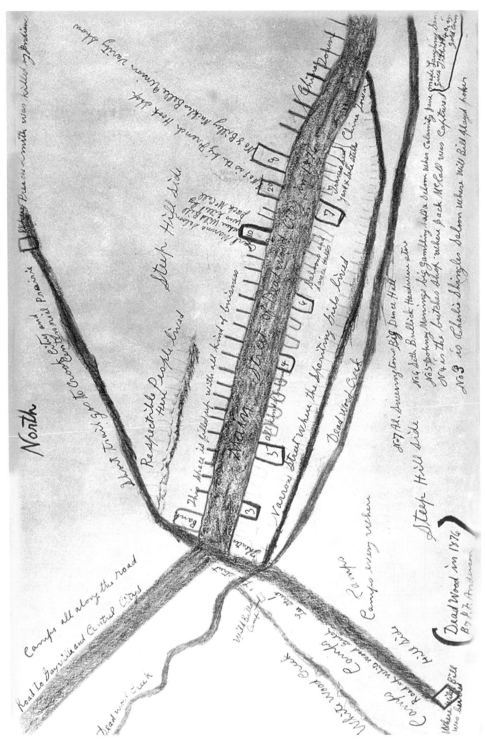

Deadwood's main street in 1876 as remembered by White Eye Anderson. (Courtesy of the late Raymond W. Thorp.)

Main Street, Deadwood in 1876. (Courtesy South Dakota State Historical Society.)

between Deadwood and Cheyenne.

Just before they departed for Deadwood, Joseph "White Eye" Anderson and his brother Charles appeared. "White Eye" (a burning buffalo chip had left his eyebrow permanently white) had met Wild Bill some years before and they both welcomed the reunion. The Andersons were invited to join the Utter-Hickok train which left late in the month and stopped at Fort Laramie on June 30. John Hunton, a post trader, recorded their visit in his diary. In later years he also expressed doubt that there was anything between Hickok and Martha Jane Cannary ("Calamity Jane") who joined the train at Fort Laramie at the Army's request (she had been confined in the guardhouse

for being drunk and disorderly), together with a number of other prostitutes and camp followers.[1]

The Army suggested that they delay their departure pending the arrival of others to join them so that they would number over a hundred for protection should they encounter warlike Sioux. The Utter-Hickok train passed through Custer City early in July. Ten years later, on July 28, 1886, an individual signing himself "Mack," and writing in the *Black Hills Daily Pioneer*, recalled that Wild Bill was accompanied by a "crew of depraved women," and that he himself was remembered by the people of Custer City as a "bum" and a "hard citizen who sought only the lower strata of society for associates."

According to White Eye Anderson (in a manuscript in the possession of his daughter which she copied for the present writer) the Hickok-Utter train met up with Buffalo Bill and a detachment of the Fifth Cavalry at Sage Creek (also known as Hat Creek) on July 6, 1876. Anderson claimed that Cody offered him a job as a scout for $100 a month, but Hickok dissuaded him. The inference being that Cody and Hickok pointedly ignored each other having fallen out when Cody claimed as his own adventures and scrapes that should have been credited to Hickok. In fact, it was not that way at all. Interviewed by a reporter from the *Roch-*

Joseph "White Eye" Anderson and his friend Yankee Judd photographed at Leadville, Colorado, circa 1879 by J. T. Needles. (Courtesy of the late Raymond W. Thorp.)

ester *Democrat & Chronicle* which appeared on September 18, 1876, Cody was asked if the story that he and Wild Bill "were bitter enemies, and were looking for each other on the plains" were true. Cody replied, "That is a bad error. Bill and I were friends always. There was but one time when he felt bad towards me, and that was from jealousy, when I was appointed chief of scouts over him by General Sheridan. I used to be under him as chief, and naturally he felt it a little. No, Bill and I were the best of friends . . . He had been in a great many fights and killed a great many men, but I never knew of his killing a man when the law and justice were not on his side. I met him on his way to the Black Hills . . . we were nooning on Sage Creek, and we talked for two hours telling of old times." Cody's long lost (or ignored) comment on his relationship with

White Eye Anderson, who accompanied Wild Bill to Deadwood, demonstrates how Wild Bill used the reverse draw. In his memoirs, he described Hickok's use of Colt's Navy model conversions. The photographs were posed by Anderson in 1940. (Courtesy of the late Raymond W. Thorp and William B. Secrest.)

Wild Bill dispells any hint of bad feelings.

The Utter-Hickok train arrived at Deadwood about July 12. The Utters and Wild Bill established a campsite on Whitewood Creek, leaving the remainder of their companions to seek campsites of their own. Calamity Jane and the other women, however, set course for Main Street.

In Deadwood, Wild Bill enjoyed a higher degree of anonymity than he was used to, which he welcomed. But this did not prevent people from wondering what might happen should anyone get ideas about employing him in some kind of law enforcement capacity. Hickok, however, is reported to have denied any such intention. On the contrary, he just wished to be allowed to prospect for gold or gamble in the hope of making sufficient money either to return to his wife in Ohio or to persuade her to join him out west.

In hindsight, we now know that he had a premonition of his impending fate and on August 1, the day before his death, he penned a short but poignant note to his wife telling

Stanley Morrow photographed Deadwood in the late 1870s, by which time it was expanding rapidly. (Courtesy of the University of South Dakota Museum.)

her that if "such should be we never meet again, while firing my last shot, I will gently breathe the name of my wife, Agnes, and with wishes even for my enemies, I will make the plunge and try to swim to the other shore."

Later, in the evening of August 1, Hickok and a young man named Bill Sutherland played poker. Only later was it discovered that his real

John, alias Jack McCall, is shown in this sketch by the author based on contemporary descriptions. (Sketched by Joseph G. Rosa.)

Colonel George May, McCall's prosecutor, from a family tintype that has suffered from the ravages of time. It is the only known image of May. (Courtesy Morgan A. Thomas.)

name was John McCall, commonly called "Jack." Carl Mann was later to testify that when Jack lost he was $16.50 short when it came time for him to pay up. Hickok agreed to await payment and offered him money for his supper or breakfast, but McCall refused it.

The following afternoon, (August 2, 1876) Hickok sat in on a leisurely poker game with three friends in the No. 10 Saloon on Main Street beginning at about one o'clock. Hickok had always made a practice of positioning himself with his back against the wall where he could have a full over-

view of the activities in a room. But this time, having joined the game after the "wall seat" had been taken, he reluctantly took a seat facing the wall with the bar at his left and back.

The poker game continued, rounds of drinks were served, and three hours passed amid the aroma of kerosene lamps, whiskey, and tobacco. At about 4:00 Bill was dealt an impressive hand of cards, two aces and two eights, that may have distracted him from his surroundings. If Bill's temporary absorption with his hand caused him to relax his usual vigilance, it was a fatal error.

This photograph has hung in the Old Style Bar at Deadwood for many years and is purported to be the only known image of Jack McCall. However, it has no provenance and bears no resemblance to the published descriptions of McCall. (Author's collection.)

What happened on this afternoon was covered very well by statements of eyewitness and files of material gathered on the event that were published in the February 28 and March 2, 1880 issues of the *Black Hills Daily Times:*

On August 2nd, 1876, Wild Bill was in Lewis & Mann's saloon on lower Main street, in this city, playing a game of poker with Capt. Massey [*sic*—Massie], a Missouri river pilot, Charley Rich and Cool [*sic*—Carl] Mann, one of the proprietors. The game had been in progress about three hours, and at about 4 o'clock, p.m. a man came in and passed up to the bar. Bill was sitting with his back to, and about five feet distant from the counter. When the man came in Bill had just picked up his hand, was looking at it, and paid no attention to the new comer. The man, who proved to be Jack McCall, alias Bill Southerland (sometimes spelled Sutherland), after approaching the bar turned, and drawing a navy re-volver, placed the muzzle within two inches of Bill's head and fired. The ball entered the base of the brain, passed through the head and upper and lower jaw bones, breaking off several teeth and carrying away a large piece of the cerebellum through the wound.

The ball struck Capt. Massey, who sat opposite Bill, in the right arm [*sic*—in court at Yankton Massie said it lodged in his left arm], and broke the bone. (Massie claimed later that it was still in his arm and invited folks to shake the hand that held the ball that killed Wild Bill.)

J. W. Buel's interpretation of how Wild Bill was murdered as illustrated in his **Heroes of the Plains.** *(Author's collection.)*

George Shingle, however, who witnessed the killing, later stated that "Wild Bill was facing the bar," but perhaps he meant that it was clearly visible to his left. It now seems evident that Wild Bill sat with his back to the rear of the room because he was the last to arrive. He found that Rich occupied the seat that would give him a clear view of the front and rear doors of the saloon and a wall at this back. He asked Rich to change places, but he declined. Grudgingly, Hickok accepted the seat which placed his back to the rear door.

Many have concluded that this trait was part of his myth, but on August 10, the editor of the *Black Hills Pioneer* noted that for some unexplained reason Hickok "was not sitting with his back to a wall. This has been his rule for many years, since his career of law enforcement had developed a long list of men who swore they would shoot him at the first opportunity."

A minor but unanswered question is: Was Hickok wearing a hat when he was shot? Although many illustrations depicting his murder show him wearing his hat, a common

This reconstructed bar is reported to have been built on the same spot once occupied by the original No. 10 saloon. But it is some distance from the reported site. (Author's collection.)

practice, none of the witnesses mentioned him wearing a hat. The question was prompted by a statement made in the Cheyenne *Daily Leader* of August 15, 1876, that the hat "worn by Wild Bill when he was murdered has been brought to this city and is now in possession of Policeman Talbot." No mention was made of bloodstains which would have been present had he been wearing it. Subsequent efforts to learn if Talbot kept the hat or if it ended up in a collection have so far proved fruitless.

After McCall fired he turned on the crowd and ordered them to file out. Once in the street he defied attempts to arrest him, but eventually gave himself up and demanded a trial. With no legally empowered body to make an arrest or take charge of the prisoner, the citizens decided to organize their own court. A coroner was appointed who empaneled a jury, and held an inquest on the body of Wild Bill which concluded that he had been shot by McCall.

Wild Bill Hickok had played his last hand and had died from a bullet, but not one fired during a gun-

fight. He had been murdered in cold blood.

In his review of the events surrounding Hickok's death, the editor of the *Times* made no mention of Wild Bill's actual poker hand when he was shot. Some years later the controversy began over what constituted the "Deadman's Hand" or "Aces and Eights" as dubbed by Ellis T. "Doc" Pierce in the 1920's. The accepted version is that the cards were the ace of spades, the ace of clubs, two black eights (clubs and spades), and either the jack of diamonds or the queen of diamonds as the "kicker." Yet the

*Captain William R. Massie in later years and reproduced in the Saint Louis, Missouri, **Republic** of February 6, 1910, to accompany his obituary. (Courtesy the late Raymond W. Thorp.)*

Many later expressed the opinion that McCall was the tool of others who wished Hickok out of the way, but were too cowardly to tackle him themselves. According to Leander Richardson, rumor was rife that Hickok was a marked man because he would not join the crooked gamblers anxious to fleece the miners. In a report to the *Denver News* (and copied by the St. Paul, Minnesota, *Pioneer Press and Tribune* of September 8, 1876), he declared that:

recollections of a star witness to the shooting, Harry "Sam" Young, has failed to receive the attention it deserves. Young, the bartender, testified that he had just given Hickok $15 in poker chips after Captain Massie beat him on the hand, and on returning to the bar heard a shot and turned to see McCall standing behind Hickok, gun in hand. In his book, *Hard Knocks* published in 1915, Young reported that Massie beat Hickok's "four sevens" with a King; but he made no reference to "aces and eights" or "the dead man's hand."

There were a dozen or more men in Deadwood who wanted to kill Wild Bill because he would not 'stand-in' with them on any 'deadbeat' games, but not one man among them all dared to pick a quarrel with him. They were all waiting to get a chance to shoot him in the back. And it was this clique who got Sutherland [McCall] clear of the charge, whereupon he took the first opportunity of getting out of town. The man charged with the murder has a most repulsive visage, and it would require no very keen imagination to picture him as the twin brother of Darwin's Missing Link.

Richardson's comments received support from others, among them the editor of the *Black Hills Pioneer* who declared on August 10, 1876, that Wild Bill was probably "the only man we have yet had in our midst who had the courage and other qualifications to bring some semblance of order to the lawless element of our camp. The fact that he was killed by one of the sorriest specimens of humanity to be found in the Hills is significant."

The *Times* continued:

A sheriff, judge and prosecuting attorney were elected by the crowd, three men were sent out in different directions to notify the miners of the murder, and request their attendance at the trial next day.

Col. Langrishe, lessee of McDaniels theatre, tendered the use of that building, and at 9 o'clock on the morning of August 3rd, Joseph Brown, the sheriff, came into court with the prisoner. F.J. [*sic*—W. L.] Kuykendall, the pro tempore judge, addressed he crowd, telling them the court was purely a self-constituted one, but that in the discharge of his duty he would be governed by justice, and trust to them for a ratification of his acts. His remarks were greeted with hand clappings of approval. The prisoner was then led forward and seated upon the right hand side of the judge, upon the stage.

His appearance was not prepossessing, his head a narrow one in the part usually occupied by the intellectual portion of the brain, while the animal portion was unusually large, was covered with a dense growth of chestnut hair; a small sandy mustache around a sensual mouth, and the coarse double chin was partially hidden by a stiff goatee. The nose was a stub, his eyes were crossed, and his general appearance was that of a bravo.

The selection of a jury consumed the forenoon, as it was difficult to find a man who had not expressed an opinion, although but few in the panel had heard of the murder until a few hours before.

A hundred names had been selected, each name written upon a piece of paper, and placed in a hat. They were well shaken, and the committee appointed for that purpose drew them out one at a time. The party answering to the name came forward, was examined by the judge touching his fitness to serve as a juror. Ninety-two names were called before the jury was made up, which consisted of J. J. Bumps, L. D. Brokow, J. H. Thompson, C. Whitehead, Geo. S. Hopkins, J. F. Cooper, Alex Travis, K. F. Towle, John E. Thompson, L. A. Judd, Edward Burke and John Mann. The jury was sworn, assigned their seats, and the testimony for the prosecution begun.

August 2, 1876

Number 10 Saloon

Deadwood,
Dakota Territory

*There are many descriptions of
how Hickok died, but not much
attention has been paid to the
layout of the No. 10 Saloon. This
reconstruction is based on
witness statements and other
references. Nuttall & Mann's No.
10 Saloon was typical of those
found in mining camps and
cattle towns.*

*George Shingle, in evidence at
the Yankton trial, said that "the
room where the bar was, was
twenty-four feet wide. The bar
took up 8 feet of the room and
was twenty feet long. I was
standing at the end of the bar.
The room was about eighty feet
long . . ." There were stools and a
few tables dotted around. There
was a front door and a back door
with one or a couple of windows,
which provided the only natural
lighting, so kerosene lamps often
burned night and day.*

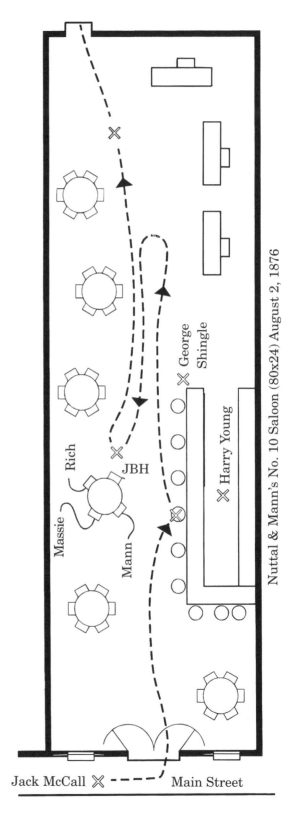

George Shingle

Harry Young

Massie

Rich

JBH

Mann

Nuttal & Mann's No. 10 Saloon (80x24) August 2, 1876

Jack McCall ✕ — — — Main Street

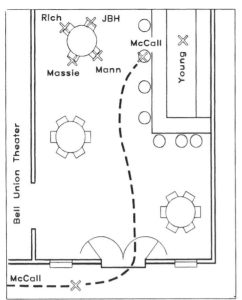

4:00 pm, August 2, 1876: Hickok was playing poker with Rich, Massie, and Mann. Hickok's back was not against the wall as was his practice; Rich had already occupied that seat. McCall enters unnoticed and takes a seat at the bar.

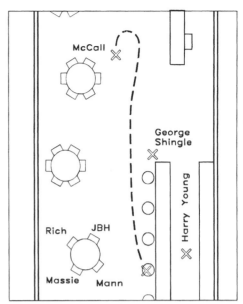

4:05 pm: McCall gets up from his stool at the bar, and walks to the back of the saloon as if he were going out the back door. He stops in the rear and hesitates.

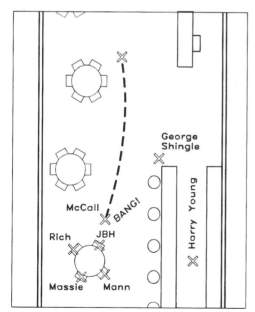

4:06 pm: McCall walks to within arm's length of Hickok and shoots him in the head. Bill dies immediately holding a hand of aces and eights.

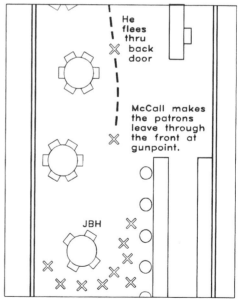

4:07 pm: McCall makes all of those in the saloon go out the front door into the street at gunpoint. He then leaves through the rear door.

John L. Pennington, Governor of Dakota Territory, who joined those anxious to seek a reprieve for McCall. (Courtesy South Dakota State Historical Society.)

The first witness called was Charles Rich, who stated that he was in the saloon on August 2nd; was at the table playing poker with Wild Bill and others, when the defendant came into the room, walked up behind Bill and placed a pistol to the back of his head and fired, saying, "take that." Bill fell to the floor without saying a word.

Samuel [Harry]Young stated that he was at work in the saloon, had just given Bill $15 worth of checks and was returning behind the bar when he heard the report of a pistol, turned around and saw the pris-

oner at the back of Bill's chair with a pistol in his hand, and heard him say "take that."

Cool Mann, one of the proprietors of the saloon, stated that he was in the poker game, noticed the commotion and saw the prisoner shoot Wild Bill. The prosecution here closed.

P. H. Smith was then called for the defense, and said that he had been in the employ of McCall four months; that he was not a quarrelsome man, and that he had always considered him a man of good character; that he had been acquainted with Wild Bill in Cheyenne, and that he had a bad reputation, and had been a terror in every place he had ever lived in.

H. H. Pickens had known the defendant four years, and believed him to be a quiet, peaceable man. Wild Bill's reputation as a shooter was very bad. He was quick in using his gun, and never missed his man, and had killed quite a number of persons in different parts of the country.

Ira Ford had known McCall about a year, and, like the rest of the boys, he would go on a spree. Bill had the reputation of being a brave man, who could, and would shoot quicker than any man in the west, and always got away with his man.

Several other witnesses were called to prove McCall's previous good character, but no attempt was made to show that he had ever seen Wild Bill before.

McCall then came forward to make his statement. With his right hand in the bosom of his shirt, his head thrown back, and in a harsh, repulsive voice, with a bulldog sort of bravado, he said: "Men, I have but a few words to say. Wild Bill killed my brother and I killed him. Wild Bill threatened to kill me if I ever crossed his patch. I am not sorry for what I have done. I would do the same thing over again." He then returned to his seat.

Evidence was then adduced to show that Wild Bill was a much abused man; that he never imposed on any one, and that every instance where he had killed a man he had done so in self-defense, or as an officer of the law in the discharge of his official duty. At 9 o'clock that evening the jury came in with the following verdict:

Deadwood City, Aug. 3, 1876.

We the jurors, find the prisoner, Mr. John McCall, not guilty.

Charles Whitehead,
Foreman.

The prisoner, McCall, was at once liberated, and several of the model jurymen who had played their part in the burlesque upon justice, and who had turned their bloodthirsty tiger loose upon the community, indulged in a sickening cheer, which grated

His Honor Judge Peter C. Shannon who officiated at McCall's Yankton trial. (Courtesy South Dakota State Historical Society.)

harshly upon the ears of those who heard it.

The first vote taken by the jury resulted in eleven for acquittal and one for conviction; and the single man, who desired to seek justice was so intimidated by the eleven, it is said, that he was soon ready to coincide with them in their verdict. It was proposed by one of the jury that he be fined ten or fifteen dollars and set free. . . .

After the farci[c]al trial McCall left town and went to work on a placer claim in Whitewood gulch, where he remained until California Joe [Moses

President U.S. Grant at the time of McCall's plea for clemency. This is one of many Grant portraits reproduced in England where he was a popular figure. (Author's collection.)

twenty-four hours to get out of the country. If I meet you after that time, one of us goes under, and then turned and left, and McCall was never seen in the gulch afterwards, but soon turned up at Yankton, under arrest; and put upon trial at that place. Geo. Shingle, who is now at Sturgis City in this county in the livery business, was an eyewitness to the shooting, but left Deadwood on the evening of the excitement, and therefore did not appear as a witness at the original trial, but appeared in answer to the summons, and there told his story of the murder. . . .

Milner], one of Bill's old friends, heard of the murder. He came in, and learning where McCall was, heeled himself and went down to see him. When he arrived at the place he seated himself on the bank, and when he caught the eye of his enemy, he motioned him to come to him. Seeing that Joe had the drop on him he came to the front. Youngster, said Joe, you and I have never met before; you have killed my best friend—murdered him, and the country is not big enough to hold us both. I don't want to murder you, and will give you just

McCall's subsequent arrest following his pursuit by Colonel George May, who had prosecuted him at Deadwood, and his trial and execution at Yankton is well covered elsewhere, but several points raised in the above account need some comment. The most important being the statement that McCall was armed with a "Navy revolver" when he shot Wild Bill. At the Yankton trial George Shingle stated that it was a "Sharps'" improved revolver; but Carl Mann also declared that it was a "Navy" pistol. This is particularly pertinent when we remember that a Colt's Single Action Army Revolver (a "Peacemaker" serial no. 2079), purported to be the pistol used by McCall, was auctioned in England in

1993. But its provenance was flawed.[2]

Other alleged pistols said to have been used by McCall were publicized in the early years of this century. Typical of these was one mentioned in the Summer 1930 issue of *Trails of the Northwoods*. Raymond W. Thorp contributed an article on "The Pistol *that* Killed Wild Bill" which included a declaration dated January 1921 by one Jean LaDuye to Dr. H. S. Rowlett of Maryville, Missouri, stating that he owned the pistol used by McCall. It was a nickel-plated Smith & Wesson in .38 caliber serial numbered 27780, patented in 1863 but marked "Reissue July 26, 1871." McCall is said to have paid $15 dollars for it and dropped it after the shooting. It was picked up by a man named Al Craig who gave it to LaDue in appreciation of his help during an illness.

Dr. Rowlett accepted the story and so did Mr. Thorp who, despite his knowledge of Hickok, evidently did not realize that its provenance was flawed.

In its description of McCall, the *Times* makes mention of his "coarse double chin" being partially hidden by a "stiff goatee." This was not mentioned in the otherwise graphic description of McCall which appeared in the Chicago *Inter-Ocean* of August 17, 1876. Despite several claims to

General W. H. Beadle, one of McCall's counsels at his Yankon trial. (Courtesy South Dakota State Historical Society.)

the contrary, no authenticated photographs of McCall have come to light.

In criticizing the jury's behavior, the *Times'* report again prompts the question: why would a jury sworn to render an honest verdict spend an hour and thirty minutes deliberating and then, despite overwhelming evidence of premeditated murder, find the defendant not guilty? Are we to believe that they really did accept his plea of revenge for his nonexistent brother? And who was the lone individual who voted against the verdict

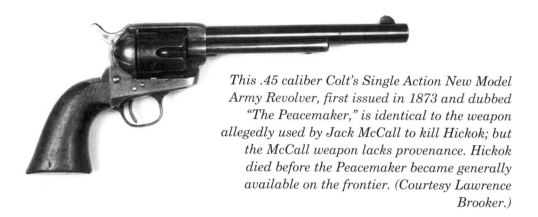

This .45 caliber Colt's Single Action New Model Army Revolver, first issued in 1873 and dubbed "The Peacemaker," is identical to the weapon allegedly used by Jack McCall to kill Hickok; but the McCall weapon lacks provenance. Hickok died before the Peacemaker became generally available on the frontier. (Courtesy Lawrence Brooker.)

until he was persuaded otherwise? Some believe it was John Mann; but conjecture is not proof.

Also, it is not generally known that the foreman, Charles Whitehead, was a special correspondent for the Kansas City *Times*, in the Hills to cover the gold rushes. Although an intensive search of that paper has failed to find a report of the trial under his byline, an examination of the city directories revealed that he was the paper's city editor. The allegation that the jury were bribed to bring in their "Not Guilty" verdict by a group of interested gamblers fearful that Hickok might become city marshal, may be linked to McCall's claim that John Varnes, a noted gambler, who had been faced down by Hickok, persuaded Jack to kill Hickok. The rumor was refuted on November 18, when the *Times* published a letter from deputy U. S. Marshal H. C. Ash. Writing from Deadwood on November 12, Ash declared that no warrant had been issued for the arrest of Varnes as was reported. Varnes himself left the Hills at about this time, and no further effort was made to subpoena him.

There was, however, another less sinister reason to explain the jury's verdict which may relate to the illegal status of Deadwood and the "self constituted" status of the "court." Had the "court" found him guilty, would he have been hanged or sent to Yankton, where there was legal jurisdiction? Those angered by the verdict would probably have preferred that McCall be hanged at Deadwood; but the editor of the *Pioneer* was obviously correct when on September 9 he wrote that any future homicides should be handled by the resident deputy U.S. Marshal who would "take the offender to Yankton, where he will have justice meted out to him in proportion to the crime."

One very important detail missing from the Yankton *Press and*

Dakotaian which covered his legal trial in great depth, was McCall's comments to the court just before sentence was passed. This was discovered in the *Black Hills Pioneer* of January 20, 1877, which cited the *Dakota Herald*. During the trial, Captain Massie claimed that some days before the actual shooting, he "saw the defendant come into the same room a day or two before and around behind Bill and pull his pistol about two thirds out. There was a young man with him who put his arm around the defendant and walked him towards the back door." That statement was not challenged by the defense (and neither does it seem that Massie thought to tell Wild Bill of McCall's actions); but according to the *Herald*, McCall denied it:

. . . . Jack McCall was asked if he had anything to say, why the penalty of death should not be passed upon him. He replied that he had a few things to say about the trial and proceeded to correct some alleged misstatements made by Capt. Massie of his going into the saloon a few days before the shooting of Wild Bill, stepping behind him and partly pulling out his pistol, was not true. He stated further that he was drunk at the time of the murder and had no clear conception of the lamentable occurrence. He had been drinking all that day, and went into the saloon where Wild Bill and others were playing cards. He remembered only going into the saloon and standing at the bar drinking when his mind went into a daze. He knew nothing further until he was awakened after a time and told that he had got himself in a bad scrap[e]. He was advised to get out of the trouble by representing that Wild Bill had killed his brother in Kansas and he did make that defense before a jury of citizens impaneled to pass upon his case. The truth was that he had never known Wild Bill, and had seen him only twice before. He wanted a new trial and thought that in justice he ought to have it. He said that his name was not Jack McCall, but he had assumed that name when leaving his old home while yet a boy, so that his parents might not know of his actions or whereabouts. These were all the remarks he had to make.

Among the interested spectators in the public gallery was Wild Bill's brother Lorenzo who had arrived late in November and remained during the whole trial. His niece Ethel Hickok told the writer that when Lorenzo was allowed to speak to McCall (we believe after the trial) he intimated that he had been bribed to kill Wild Bill, but refused to say anything further or show any remorse. This disgusted and angered Lorenzo, and in later years the name McCall was rarely uttered in his presence.

Following the passing of the death sentence, McCall's defense tried every means possible to secure a pardon or commutation of his sentence. Even the territorial governor, John L. Pennington, was persuaded to support their motions and reiterated McCall's and others' claim that he was drunk when he shot Wild Bill. William Pound, however, who had prosecuted at the trial, refuted this claim, and was very outspoken in his letter of February 7, 1877, addressed to the Attorney General, the Honorable Alphonso Taft. He acknowledged Taft's request that he examine the various petitions and communicate verbally with the trial judge, Chief Justice P. C. Shannon.

The judge declined on professional grounds to interfere. Pound himself was adamant that McCall's interests had been carefully guarded by the Court. As for the allegations concerning Hickok's character made in court and in the petitions, Pound declared:

A reference to the indictment will show that both his real name and the alias of "Wild Bill" were used in it. But the name "Wild Bill" had been given to him and fastened upon him so that he was really better known by that than any other, and without any discredit to himself. It is a part of the history of the war, that this man, by reason of his fearless and efficient service as a Union Scout among the guer[r]illas of Missouri, Arkansas and Eastern Kansas, and by his contests with these same guer[r]illas even after the war closed, when they so persistently pursued him, won this name of "Wild Bill," and he certainly had no reason, during his life to be ashamed of it. The same policy pursued him even to the Black Hills, his old enemies giving him a bad name whenever and wherever they dared do it. Although the evidence was clearly inadmissible in a case like this, where the prisoner sought the deceased, and while in no danger, shot him from behind, I did not object to, and the court permitted testimony as to the character of the deceased for violence. One witness, for some years a passenger conductor on the Kansas Pacific Railway, who knew him there, ten years or more ago, and who had known him since at Cheyenne and in the Black Hills, said he was not a quarrelsome man and never quarrelled unless forced into it. Other witnesses gave him the same character and no one gave him a different one.

In the late 1950s I was informed that when Attorney General Taft presented McCall's papers to President Grant, he stared at them for some moments, removed his cigar from his mouth, and asked if "Wild Bill" was the same man mentioned by former Union Army officers who held him in high regard? Taft said that it was. Grant looked up. "Clemency denied," he said, clamping his cigar back between his teeth and returning to matters of state.

It is a good yarn but, as I suspected, it is just that, for correspondence with the National Archives, Kansas City Branch, confirmed that "pardons are not necessarily put before the President." In fact, even had Grant been personally involved, there was no way that he would allow personal feelings to interfere. Rather, he would be guided solely by Taft's review of the evidence.[3]

McCall's petition was refused and he was hanged on March 1, 1877.

Notes

1. William B. Secrest (Editor), *I Buried Hickok: The Memoirs of White Eye Anderson* (College Station, Texas, 1980), 92-99; L. G. ("Pat") Flannery, *John Hunton's Diary (1876-77)* (Lingle, Wyoming, 1958) which includes Hunton's "Recollections" of Calamity Jane, 109-111; James D. McLaird, "Calamity Jane's Diary and Letters, Story of a Fraud," *Montana: The Magazine of Western History* 45:4 (Autumn/Winter, 1995), 20-35.

2. A personal examination of the weapon's provenance and associated materials, kindly provided by the British auctioneers, convinced me that the pistol was spurious. As for the "Sharps; improved revolver" alleged by Shingle to be the murder weapon, this suggests the model patented by Sharps in 1871, but no long-barreled specimens are known, and the standard short-barreled version is uncommon. Further confusion was caused by Shingle's mention of a piece of buckskin sewn to the stock, which suggests a repair to an older weapon (A. W. F. Taylerson, *The Revolver 1865-1888*. London, 1966, 247-48, and in correspondence with Joseph G. Rosa, May 13, 1999).

3. Joseph G. Rosa. *Alias Jack McCall: A Pardon or Death?* Kansas City, Missouri, 1967, *passim;* see also: Joseph G. Rosa, "Jack McCall Assassin: An Updated Account of his Yankton Trial, Plea for Clemency, and Execution," *The Brand* Book, Vol. 32, No. 1 (Winter 1997/1998), The English Westerners' Society, London, 1999; Diana L. Duff, National Archives—Central Plains Region, Kansas City, Missouri, to Joseph G. Rosa, August 3, 1998.

Chapter Eleven

LAID TO REST

It may not have been "a shot heard around the world," when Jack McCall shot Wild Bill Hickok from behind on the afternoon of Wednesday, August 2, 1876, but its echo has ricocheted around the West ever since. For Hickok's death not only brought to an end the life of a fascinating individual, but it inspired a legend that defies all attempts to dispel it.

The news of Wild Bill's murder had nationwide repercussions. Many doubted it—he had been reported killed on several occasions—but when it was confirmed, his family in Illinois and Kansas were devastated. In the West, he was much mourned, and his friends were quick to point out that had Hickok been given a chance for his life McCall would most certainly have lost his.

In Kansas especially, the news of Hickok's murder aroused a great deal of interest. On August 17, 1876, the Hays City *Ellis County Star* asked, ". . . is this the long-looked for ending of the career of one who deserved a better fate . . . While here he killed several men; but all their acquaintances agreed that he was justified in so doing. He never provoked a quarrel, and was a generous, gentlemanly fellow . . . had the fellow that shot him given him a fair fight, and not taken the cowardly advantage that he did, Wild Bill would not have been killed." At Abilene the *Chronicle* mentioned Hickok's death but relied upon a reprint of an article from the St. Louis *Globe-Democrat* to outline his deeds and accomplishments.

For the Hickok family, the weeks immediately following his death were fraught with speculation, anger, and great sorrow. His sister, Lydia, writing from Oberlin, Kansas to the folks at Troy Grove asked, "Is it true? It seems awful hard as [to] be true . . . .

An early view by Morrow of Sherman Street, Deadwood, circa 1876-77. (Courtesy University of South Dakota, Vermillion.)

I do wish I was there with Mother. Now if this is true it will nearly kill her [.] Oh dear I feel so bad down here alone[.] I would much rather he had been killed with Custer."

Even as McCall's Deadwood trial was in progress, Charlie Utter, much affected by his friend's death, set about organizing his funeral. The press of the *Black Hills Pioneer* printed the following notice which was widely distributed amongst the miners:

Wild Bill's grave photographed shortly after his burial. Reproduced many times (this version comes from a steroscopic print), the original photographer has not been identified. (Author's collection.)

*This photograph of two men at Wild Bill's grave circa 1877 has rarely been cred-
ited to the original photographer, and neither have the pair been properly identified. The plate was mde by N. N. Maguire and was copied as a woodcut in his
book,* **The Coming Empire: A Complete and Reliable Treatise on the Black
Hills, Yellowstone, and Big Horn Regions,** *published in 1878. He persuaded
"Colorado Charley" and "Arapaho Joe" to pose beside the grave as "prominent
features." Utter is the seated man at the right. (Author's collection.)*

Funeral Notice—Died, in Deadwood, Black Hills, August 2, 1876, from the effects of a pistol shot, J. B. Hickock (Wild Bill) formerly of Cheyenne, Wyoming. Funeral services will be held at Charlie Utter's camp, on Thursday afternoon, August 3d, at 3 o'clock P.M. All are respectfully invited to attend.

On March 2, 1880, in his "Early Days" reminiscences, the editor of the *Black Hills Daily Times* described the funeral:

At the appointed hour a large number of people gathered there. Charlie had spared no expense to make the funeral as fine as possible. A handsome coffin had been procur[r]ed, covered with black cloth and richly ornamented with silver mountings, and in it lay Wild Bill a picture of perfect repose. His long chestnut hair, parted in the middle, hung in waving ringlets over his broad shoulders; his face was cleanly shaven, excepting his drooping moustache, which shaded a mouth which in death almost seemed to smile; the arms were folded over the stilled breast, which enclosed a heart that had beaten with regular pulsation amid the most startling scenes of blood and violence. The body was dressed in a complete suit of black broadcloth, and by his side lay his trusty rifle, which in life had been prized above all other things.

A clergyman read an impressive funeral service, which was attentively listened to by the audience, the lid of the coffin was closed, and the procession moved up to the burying ground on the hill where a grave had been prepared, and soon all that was earthly of Wild Bill had been returned to mother earth . . .

Several sources state that the first headboard inscription over Hickok's grave was carved into the tree stump at his head:

A brave man,
The victim of an Assassin,
J. B. Hickock (Wild Bill),
Aged 48 years,
Murdered by Jack McCall,
August 2, 1876.

By early 1877, however, Charlie Utter had replaced it with a large board, worked on by a sign writer, that remained in place for some years before being replaced by several stone monuments. Each summer, however, visitors to Hickok's grave on Mount Moriah are able see a close copy of the original board[1] which is placed inside the wire cage protecting the grave which reads:

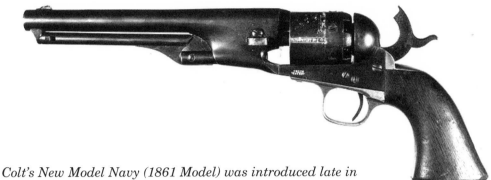

Colt's New Model Navy (1861 Model) was introduced late in 1860. In appearance it resembles the New Model Army revolver of 1860. Utilizing the same forgings as used on the Army barrel, Colt machined them down to Navy size. Despite its streamlined appearance, however, the 1861 Model Navy was never as popular as its legendary octagonal-barreled predecessor, the Model 1851 Navy. (Courtesy of the Kansas State Historical Society.)

Notes

WILD BILL
J. B. HICKOCK
Killed by the Assassin
JACK MCCALL
DEADWOOD BLACK HILLS
August 2, 1876.
Pard we will
meet again
in the happy
Hunting grounds
to part no more
Good Bye
COLORADO
CHARLIE
C. H. UTTER.[2]

1. A very old full-size copy of this board is also to be found fixed to the wall of the Olde Style Bar in present-day Deadwood, which houses a number of Wild Bill related relics.

2. In his *Heroes of the Plains* (p. 200) Buel correctly pointed out that Hickok was 39 and not 48 years of age at the time of his death. However his figure of "39 years, 10 months and 12 days" should have read 39 years, two months and six days.

Chapter Twelve

MOUNT MORIAH:
THE FINAL RESTING PLACE

Sightseers abounded in the Black Hills in the three years following Wild Bill's death. Almost daily someone stopped by his grave to pay his or her respects, or simply to copy Charlie Utter's headboard inscription.

One visit that was widely publicized, was that of his wife, Agnes. On September 8, 1877, she stood alone for some time beside his grave before returning head bowed to her friends. Later she announced that it was to remain undisturbed and that thanks to Buffalo Bill and others a monument would be erected. Despite her declared love for Wild Bill and her letter to his mother dated November 12, 1876, in which she wrote that "the longer he is dead the worse I feel," less than a year later she had remarried.

According to records at Cheyenne, Wyoming, on her return from the trip to Deadwood accompanied by one George Carson, she married him on September 27, 1877. How long the marriage lasted is uncertain, for he soon disappeared (it has not been confirmed if they were divorced, separated, or if and when he died). When Buel interviewed her in the early 1880s, he described her as Mrs. Hickok, the name Agnes was known by when she died in 1907.[1]

In August 1879, two years after Agnes's visit to the Hills, the expanding city of Deadwood made it necessary for land then occupied as a grave site to be included, so preparations were made to move Hickok's body and others to a new cemetery on Mount Moriah. Colorado Charlie again took charge of the arrangements, paid for a new plot, and obtained the assistance of John S. McClintock, Lewis Schoenfield, and William Austin to dig up Hickok's

J. H. Riordan, the sculptor, stands beside Bill's tombstone that was erected in 1891. (Courtesy of Mary Kopco and Carol Reif of the Adams Museum.)

coffin for reburial. They began this chore promptly at sunrise on September 3. Upon removal of the coffin Charlie opened it for one last view of Wild Bill. When Bill's body was examined, it was found to be in a perfect state but it was petrified, appar-ently due to chemicals in the soil. The *Times* on March 4, 1880, recounted what happened:

. . . . It was a sad sight to the eyes of the friends. There was a scarcely perceptible change in the body, except-

Hickok's grave is in section 1, lot 71 of Mount Moriah cemetery. Calamity Jane (Martha Jane Cannary) is buried in lot 70. (Courtesy of Mary Kopco and Carol Reil, Adams Museum.)

ing a darker color of the face. There was the shattered wound in the right cheek, made by the cruel bullet which took his life, but the countenance bore a tranquil look, as though the wearer was glad to escape a world in which there was nothing but buffet and anxiety to him. The lips wore a placid appearance—a smile of peace, the grateful contour of content.

The extraordinary weight of the body caused them to examine it more closely than they otherwise would, when they discovered that petrification had commenced. The hair still bore its silken lustre, but the flesh was so changed that it had become as hard as wood. The weight of the body at interment was one hundred and sixty pounds but at the exhumation was double that weight.

The carbine that was buried with him was in a perfect state of preservation. After taking a lock of hair the lid of the coffin was again screwed down and the remains taken to Moriah cemetery, where they now repose, in a lot purchased by Charley Utter. It is the intention of his friends to erect a handsome marble

This enlargment of the photograph of Utter at Hickok's grave in 1877 is the only known photograph of Colorado Charlie. (Author's collection.)

This pen-and-ink drawing of Colorado Charlie Utter made by Janet Lange and published in an article by Louis L. Simonin "Le Far-West American" in the French magazine, **Le Tour du Monde,** *is the only other image of him. (Author's collection.)*

head stone at the grave, with the proper inscriptions. The stone has been ordered, and will be erected this coming season.[2]

In describing Hickok's final resting place, the editor of the *Times,* on March 4, declared that the:

. . . rough sounds of a border settlement, with its dangers and privations, has given place to the melody of a maiden's voice, and other generations, like the ocean waves which obliterate the sand marks on the beach, has destroyed the vestiges of the early settlement, and points to

Calamity Jane (Martha Jane Cannary) as she appeared in about 1880. (Earle collection.)

C. E. FINN,   LIVINGSTON, MONT.

Wild Bill's grave as the spot where sleeps a hero pioneer, a man whose heart was as gentle as a child's and as brave as God would make it. If he had faults, they were tempered with so much compassion and affection that we lose sight of them entirely.

Buel evidently read that passage and was so impressed that he copied part of it (with some changes and no acknowledgment) in his *Heroes of the Plains.*

Despite the editor of the *Times'* confidence that Wild Bill would be left in peace, there were those who thought otherwise. Attempts to exhume Wild Bill for exhibition in a freak show were forestalled by Charlie Utter and the Hickok family. In April 1880, Lorenzo arrived in Deadwood to frustrate any further attempts. Later, Captain Jack Crawford and others would contribute toward the several monuments that were erected. Unfortunately, over the years they were vandalized and ultimately destroyed by souvenir seekers.[3]

Today, Wild Bill sleeps on, undisturbed except for the thousands of tourists who flock into Deadwood (many attracted by the state approved gambling) who make a point of visiting his grave. To some it is simply a relic of a bygone era, to be photographed standing beside it for the family album. But for others it is the closest they will come to meeting a man whose legendary status as a pistoleer, peace officer and "civilizer" keeps him at the forefront of America's folk heroes.

In reviewing Hickok's legendary status, the editor of the Yankton *Press and Dakotaian* in his issue of March 1, 1877, remarked that though "his life was bloody and adventurous, yet he was the champion of the weak and oppressed; and if he was not a paragon of excellence, he was at least a man of brave impulses."

A sentiment shared by the editor of the Laramie, Wyoming, *Daily Chronicle* and cited by the Leavenworth, Kansas, *Appeal* of August 25, 1876:

Poor Bill! He died just as he has expected for years past, "with his boots on; shot in the back." But he was not a lawless character, by any means, and those who would so brand him did not know the man whose memory, by reason of the protection he afforded peaceable citizens when desperadoes made life and property insecure, will ever be cherished by many . . . with feelings of sincere affection.

Notes

1. Laramie County Record Books, Book C, 21, discloses that a marriage certificate was issued to George Carson and Agnes Hickok on September 27, 1877, and returned for filing the next day.

2. Charley Utter having paid for Hickok's new grave kept a vigil over it for years to stop ghouls from the East digging him up for public exhibition (see Agnes Wright Spring, *Colorado Charley, Wild Bill's Pard* (Boulder, Colorado, 1968) for a detailed account).

3. The remains of one of the original monuments is now housed in the Adams Museum at Deadwood. Plans to place a bronze monument over Hickok's grave have so far not reached fruition; but it would provide a better deterrent to souvenir vandals than stone!

Chapter Thirteen

WILD BILL'S RIFLE AND OTHERS

Wild Bill's reburial again focused attention on the long arms and hand guns allegedly carried by him during his 21 days in Deadwood. Long the subject of controversy, myth and speculation, some writers have even suggested that Wild Bill did not own a handgun during his period in the Black Hills. This is nonsense, of course, and earlier we examined some of the reported weapons. But such stories have created an industry of speculation. Perhaps the most publicized appeared in the Cheyenne *Daily Leader* of July 1, 1879, when it was announced that his grave had been robbed and his pistols stolen:

> His ivory handled revolvers . . . were made expressly for him and were finished in a manner unequalled by any ever before manufactured in this or any other country. It is said that a bullet from them never missed its mark. Remarkable stories are told of the dead shootist's skill with these guns. He could keep two fruit cans rolling, one in front and one behind him, with bullets fired from these firearms. This is only a sample story of the hundreds which are related of his incredible dexterity with these revolvers

The alleged grave robbery was soon scotched by Carlie Utter and others, but at various times the Adams Museum has had on display weapons purported to have been removed from his grave, among them a four-barrel Sharps derringer. In a semi-relic condition, due to being exposed to water and other corrosive elements, it was stolen from the museum some time ago.

A non-coffin acquisition was a Belgian pinfire revolver (said to have been one of a pair presented to Buf-

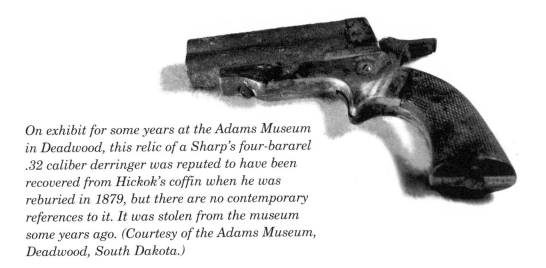

On exhibit for some years at the Adams Museum in Deadwood, this relic of a Sharp's four-bararel .32 caliber derringer was reputed to have been recovered from Hickok's coffin when he was reburied in 1879, but there are no contemporary references to it. It was stolen from the museum some years ago. (Courtesy of the Adams Museum, Deadwood, South Dakota.)

falo Bill Cody). But the most important weapon was the rifle buried with Wild Bill and removed from the coffin when he was exhumed.

John S. McClintock in his book, *Pioneer Days in the Black Hills,* claimed that Hickok had several revolvers when he arrived in Deadwood. One he claimed was a "finely carved, ivory-handled Colts forty-four caliber, model of 1850." Hickok told him that it had been the gift of Kit Carson. It had been used so much that it was worn out and liable to multiple discharge. Wild Bill apparently exchanged it for a board debt he owed one Captain Dotson (Dobson?). Since Hickok "boarded" with Charlie Utter this seems unlikely. McClintock was probably confusing the patent date of September 10, 1850, which covered certain modifications, that appeared on the cylinder of the New Model Army Revolver (commonly called the "Model 1860 Army") for a "model" definition. We suspect, however, that Mr. McClintock was repeating hearsay.

Where doubt exists or the provenance is scanty concerning some of the pistols that Hickok is supposed to have owned while at Deadwood, material relative to the rifle he carried is substantial. Here one finds contemporary references to the type and make of weapon retrieved from his coffin at his reburial in 1879.

Joseph "White-Eye" Anderson recalled that Hickok was armed with a "Big Fifty," a .56 caliber long barreled rifle that was called the Springfield single shot needle rifle. It had three bands. "When he shot a buffalo with it, it would make a hole big enough for a calf to jump through."[1] I suspect that he wrote that description from memory. The "Big Fifty" definition was attributed to the

*John S. McClintock along with William Austin, and Lewis Scoenfield assisted Colorado Charlie Utter in exhuming Wild Bill Hickok from his first grave on September 3, 1879, in order to rebury him in the Moriah Cemetery. (From McClintock's, **Pioneer Days in the Black Hills.**)*

Sharps .50 caliber Buffalo rifle brought out after Hickok's death. Nevertheless, the weapon buried with Wild Bill was in .50 caliber, and Anderson was correct in identifying it as a Springfield.

John S. McClintock, one of those who claimed to have been one of four who were present when Hickok's coffin was opened prior to reburial, stated the following in 1939 concerning Hickok's rifle:

It has been stated by the acting undertaker who was in charge of the original [first] funeral, that Wild Bill's big Sharps rifle was buried by his side. This statement the writer knows to be incorrect, as he saw the gun in the coffin when it was opened on reinterment. It was not a Sharps rifle, but a carbine, or a short cavalry, fitted into an old-fashioned Kentucky rifle breech, with the name J. B. Hickok engraved [carved] in the wood. After his death his personal effects were disposed of, and John Bradley of Spearfish, South Dakota, purchased the Sharps rifle. He used the gun for many years afterwards in hunting for wild game. Subsequently it came into possession of Allen Toomey, of Spearfish, now deceased.[2]

Since he was writing about a single gun, the "carbine rifle" in Hickok's coffin, his mistaken reference to a "Sharps purchased by Bradley" was an editorial oversight that

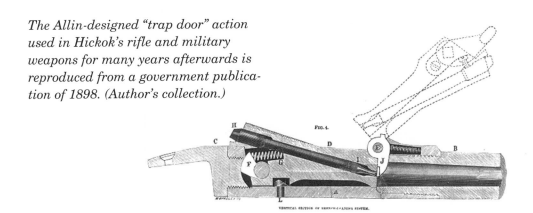

The Allin-designed "trap door" action used in Hickok's rifle and military weapons for many years afterwards is reproduced from a government publication of 1898. (Author's collection.)

was not corrected. It is apparent that he was writing of a non-Sharps rifle that was taken from Hickok's coffin, purchased by John Bradley, and subsequently acquired by Allen Toomey also from Spearfish.

Writing to me on July 15, 1956, the late Nell Perrigoue, Secretary of the Deadwood Chamber of Commerce, stated that the "Sharps rifle" owned by Mr. Bradley had been "loaned to our Museum and it was there for several years until claimed by a nephew in Louisiana." [The "nephew" was McFadden Duffy, husband of Isabell Toomey of New Orleans.] She concluded that "history is so soon distorted and there are so few records to be consulted." Miss

Perrigoue's reference to "Sharps" confirms my suspicion that no one seems to have taken much notice of the weapon otherwise they would have soon discovered that it was a Springfield.

What is not clear, of course, is how Charlie Utter, who paid for Hickok's new gravesite, and supervised his reburial, was persuaded to remove the rifle from the coffin and then part with it! Indeed, as we have noted, the *Black Hills Pioneer Times* in its report of the reburial makes no mention of the removal of the rifle, so while we know that John Bradley took possession of it, we do not know the circumstances.

As for the rifle itself, an exami-

The Hickok Rifle as it appeared when on display at Adams Memorial Hall in Deadwood, South Dakota.

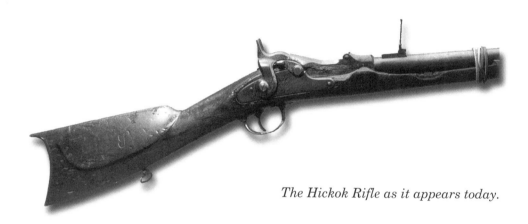

The Hickok Rifle as it appears today.

nation of it based upon photographic and documentary evidence suggests that it is a sporting version of the Springfield military rifle Model 1870 in .50-70 caliber and customized with a Kentucky rifle-style sloped butt of the type still popular on the plains in the late 1860s and early 1870s. The stock has been further customized with shaped cheek pieces on each side which would appeal to left or right-handed shooters. By actual measurement, the barrel is 29-5/8 inches long (carbine barrels were normally 20 to 24 inches in length), and is fitted with a standard leaf rear sight. The action was designed by Erskine S. Allin, Master Armorer at the Springfield Armory. This action was commonly called a "trap door" because to load or eject cartridges, the hinged breech block was tipped up and forward like a trap door. Besides the date of "1870," the action is also marked with a crossed sabers motif, and the lockplate bears the

A view of the Hickok rifle showing the separation of the retaining escutchen plate at the stock.

The initials "JB" are carved into the stock, perhaps to stand for "John Bradley."

word "Springfield" and the year 1863. This latter information means that the lock was manufactured originally for a percussion rifle; but following the Civil War, was among thousands converted from percussion to Allin's system. Between 1865 and 1873, a number of "new models" were issued, stamped with the year, and chambered for the current ammunition demanded by the military, and included any refinements to the mechanism. Therefore, the Hickok rifle complied with the demands of 1870. The ramrod, designed for percussion use, was retained, for apart from its need for cleaning purposes, sometimes spent cartridges jammed in the action and it was used to remove them.[3]

The United States Government spent a great deal of time and money experimenting with various types of rifles and carbines. By 1870, a variety of calibers and ammunition were available. A glance at contemporary publications and military manuals reveals that plainsmen and the military could use .50-70-500 or .50-70-405 Government rifle or carbine loads, or experiment themselves to get the right bullet weight and pow-

"J B Hickok" is carved into the cheekpiece of the Springfield's stock.

der ratio that suited them. (The foregoing first figure indicates that the caliber was .50, the soft lead bullet weighed 500 grains, and it was powered by 70 grains of black powder). In Hickok's case, we have no means of knowing his preference.

McCintock wrote that the name "J. B. Hickok" had been engraved on the stock (the cheek piece on the left side), when in fact it had been carved into it with a sharp knife. On the right side of the cheek piece appears a monograph or brand-like combination of "JB" (shown in the photograph above) which presumably means "John Bradley." The inspection mark "A" appears on the inside of the up-per trapdoor, and the same letter appears in front of the triggerguard.

According to Isabel Toomey Duffy, the rifle came into her family's possession via her grandfather, Daniel Toomey. He had left his native Brooklyn and set out for the Black Hills in the wake of the gold fever, and reached Deadwood Gulch before the town of Deadwood was laid out in April 1876. He worked as a carpenter in the new city and later located at Spearfish. During his short period in Deadwood he got to know Wild Bill, but was not on intimate terms with him. Nevertheless, he expressed a great admiration for the man and his exploits, and when he

Daniel Joseph Toomey of Spearfish, South Dakota, is believed to have obtained the Hickok Springfield from John Bradley at age eighteen.

Daniel Toomey with his granddaugher, Eileen Toomey, the daughter of Daniel's son, Edward.

learned that "one of the old settlers" had Hickok's rifle (presumably John Bradley), he persuaded him to sell it to him. He later gave it to his son Allen. On his death his wife loaned it to the Adams Museum where it remained as a popular exhibit until the early 1950s when Isabel requested its return to her.

James H. Earle, its present owner, has advised me that so far as he is aware, the rifle has not been taken part for many years, perhaps since Hickok himself last used it. Therefore, he is reluctant to disturb the weapon:

I cannot find a serial number on the outside of the gun and I am reluctant to take it apart since the screws and parts fit the way they are supposed to after 100 years with the proper patina and accompanying grime that comes with time. I am guessing the buttplate is brass, but it has turned a brownish color, much the same color as the stock, and it has melded and fused into the stock almost as if it were part of the wood (much as you would expect it to look if it had been left in a coffin).

Allen Toomey, son of Daniel Joseph Toomey, is pictured holding the Hickok Springfield rifle in Rapid City, South Dakota in 1934.

W. McFadden Duffy and his wife, Isabell Toomey Duffy (daughter of Allen Toomey), study the Hickok rifle in 1953 after it had been returned to the family by the Adams Memorial Hall in Deadwood.

The obvious question raised by most Hickok students would be: when did Hickok acquire this rifle? The date of 1870 precludes any plains use prior to that time, and there is little evidence of him engaging in buffalo hunts post 1869. I suspect that the answer is to be found in the last year of Hickok's life. It is not generally known that from circa June 1875 he spent time in parts of Missouri, some of it in Kansas City and the remainder at St. Louis, from where he is reported to have visited the Hills prior to his fateful and last trip. According to the St. Louis *Times* of April 2, 1876, Hickok had "just returned from the Black Hills country, and will cheerfully tell you all about it." Later that month he had already planned another expedition to the Hills, and in letters to the press, indicated that each man should have at least "one good rifle" and "200 rounds of ammunition" together with other supplies, to last for at least six months.

My conclusion, therefore, is that

Bill Duffy, son of McFaddin and Isabell Duffy, is pictured in a 1962 newspaper clipping holding the Hickok rifle.

the rifle now owned by James H. Earle and formerly by the Bradley and the Toomey families, was probably purchased by Wild Bill perhaps a year before his death, either in Cheyenne, where he lived for some time, or later in Kansas City or St. Louis, where a glance at advertisements of the time indicate that gun dealers in general were advising anyone brave or foolhardy enough to chase gold and risk Indian attack, to arm themselves with the best weapons available. Wild Bill, with good reason, chose the Springfield.

Notes

1. William Secrest, *I Buried Hickok,* 96.

2. John S. McClintock, *Pioneer Days in the Black Hills,* page 114.

3. Students of General Custer will be aware that the lack of ramrods for the cavalry carbines, and defective ammunition (which tended to jam in the chamber) contributed to his "Last Stand" at the Little Big Horn on June 25, 1876.

Chapter Fourteen

WEAPONS OF THE GUNFIGHTS

Wild Bill engaged in six known gunfights, and his authenticated victims numbered six (seven if one includes David McCanles). But in some instances others were involved, either as participants or because they were in the wrong place at the wrong time. Therefore, in providing this resume of Hickok's gunfights, we will also include others who were involved and list the known weapons used either by Hickok or his antagonists.

1861: July 12, at Rock Creek, Nebraska Territory. David C. McCanles was shot either by Hickok or Horace Wellman, the station keeper. James Woods and James Gordon, employees of McCanles were also killed. Woods is believed to have been killed by Jane Wellman with a hoe, and someone else (perhaps Hickok, or Doc Brink the Pony Express rider—depending upon which account one reads), wounded Gordon. When Gordon fled into the brush he was pursued and killed with a shotgun, but by whom has not been established.

Weapons: McCanles is reputed to have always worn two revolvers and carried a sawed-off shotgun which he kept on his saddle bow. The Wellmans had an elderly Kentucky type rifle made by Postley Nelson & Co., that some claim was owned by McCanles but left in the ranch house as a means of protection. Hickok is said to have been armed with a pair of Colt's Navy revolvers; but that has not been proved.

1865: July 21, at Springfield, Mo. Hickok and Davis K. Tutt, having fallen out over a disputed gambling debt, opened fire on each other at 75 yards. Dave turned sideways on (dueling fashion) and missed, but

Hickok's ball entered at the fifth rib on the right side and came out at the fifth rib on the left, cutting through his heart. Both men opened fire "simultaneously" according to witnesses. Hickok pleaded self-defense at his trial for manslaughter which ended in a "Not Guilty" verdict.

Weapons: We know from photographic evidence and the statement made by Colonel George Ward Nichols, that Hickok was armed with a pair of Colt's Navy revolvers. Unfortunately, Dave Tutt's "cap and ball revolver" has never been identified, but in all probably it was similar in make and model to Hickok's.

1869: August 22, at Hays City, Kansas. Bill Mulvey (or Mulrey) was shot by Hickok following a drunken orgy in which he tried to shoot bystanders.

Weapons: Mulvey's weapon is unidentified, but Hickok was armed with a pair of Colt's Navies.

1869: September 27, Hays City, Kansas. Samuel Strawhun and some cronies tried to clear out a beer saloon and threatened the lives of anyone who brought back glasses that they had removed to a vacant lot. Hickok arrived and retrieved some of the glasses, replacing them on the bar. Strawhun then threatened him—either with a pistol or a bro-

ken jagged glass. Wild Bill shot him, which met with the approval of the locals and he was exonerated by the coroner's jury.

Weapons: Hickok was armed with his two Navy pistols, but no one has speculated on Strawhun's pistol or pistols.

1870: July 17-18, Hays City, Kansas, Hickok was attacked by two Seventh Cavalry troopers, Jeremiah Lonergan and John Kile. Lonergan dragged Hickok backwards to the ground and prevented him from getting to his pistols. During the struggled, Kile thrust the barrel of his pistol into Wild Bill's ear and pulled the trigger. It misfired. Hickok had by now managed to draw a pistol. He shot Kile twice and Lonergan once in the knee. Hickok escaped the wrath of some troopers who headed for town once they heard of the shooting, by hiding out on Boot Hill prepared to sell his life dearly. Kile died later in the post hospital. The army took no official action because the troopers were involved in a drunken brawl and were not in the line of duty.

Weapons: Hickok was armed with two Navy pistols (and an 1866 Model Winchester rifle in his hotel room), while Lonergan and Kile carried regulation .44 caliber Remington New Model Army pistols (as issued to some troops of the Seventh). Unfortunately for Kile, it was not a reliable weapon, and was prone to misfire. Indeed, it was reported from Fort Laramie, Wyoming, in 1867, that twelve pistols burst and a large number of them misfired when put on trial, which made General C.C. Auger furious. Wild Bill, perhaps without realizing it, on that occasion owed his life to the Remington Arms Company!

1871: October 5, at Abilene, Kansas. Hickok and Phil Coe shot it out face-to-face and only eight feet apart. Coe is reported to have fired two shots at him and missed (one went through Hickok's coat and one hit the ground between his legs). Two of Hickok's bullets smacked into Coe's stomach and he also accidentally killed Mike Williams who ran between them and was not recognized by Hickok. Coe died three days later and his body was shipped back to Texas for burial. Hickok, meanwhile, paid for Williams's funeral and later explained to his grieving young widow what happened that fateful day.

Weapons: Hickok used a pair of Colt's Navies, but neither Coe nor Williams's' pistols were identified.

It is clear from the foregoing accounts of Hickok's gunfights and the weapons he used that the revolver or "equalizer" as some called it played a significant role in the life and sometimes the death of a gunfighter—as it did in the lives of ordinary individuals who used it in defense of self or family. Nevertheless, generations have grown up to admire, fear, and ultimately respect the weapons that gave the gunfighters purpose and made or destroyed reputations.

Colt's revolvers are now world famous, especially the Single Action Army Revolver, Model 1873, commonly called "The Peacemaker," but Hickok died before it became generally available to civilians.

Notes on the Weapons

The following notes give the contemporary evaluations of the major types of arms that were used during Hickok's era. At this time, guns were essential tools of the soldiers, frontiersmen, and homesteaders, and all guns were still in their developmental stages. Examples of these firearms are pictured in the earlier chapters of this volume.

Colt's Dragoon, Army or Holster Pistol, Model 1848

Wild Bill, according to early residents of Johnson County, Kansas, is reported to have owned or had access to a Colt's Dragoon revolver as early as 1857-58. They recalled that it was a "common feat with him to take a stand at a distance of a hundred yards from an oyster can, and with a heavy dragoon revolver send every bullet through it with unerring precision. He had not then commenced his practice upon human beings."[1] Later writers have suggested that Wild Bill shot Davis Tutt with a Dragoon, resting the barrel on a post to take aim and steady it. While we cannot discredit the Johnson County recollections, which may or may not have been embellished, there is no contemporary evidence to support the latter claim—available records indicate that Hickok was armed with a pair of Colt's Navy revolvers when he shot Tutt.

The Dragoon pistol became a legend in its own time, and owed its origin to the Mexican War (1846-48). In 1846, with the prospect of war with Mexico a grim reality, the United States Government approached Sam Colt to find out if he could supply revolving pistols for use in the coming conflict. Sam, of course, was delighted. His original Paterson Patent Fire Arms Company had gone into liquidation some years before. For although his pistols and cylinder rifles had found a ready market, especially with the United States Army, production costs and faults in the weapons'

lock-work led eventually to bankruptcy. But Sam was undeterred. Several years in the wilderness, working on mines and other futuristic projects, kept him busy until he was requested to modify his existing arms for use in the war with Mexico.

Captain Samuel Walker of the United States Mounted Rifles Regiment (and himself a former Texas Ranger under John ("Coffee") Hays) was authorized to negotiate with Colt. He listed a number of faults found with the original weapons, and encouraged Colt to improve and better his design, with the result that with Walker's help he received the government revolver contract. Eli Whitney, Jr., of Whitneyville, Connecticut, utilizing British iron and steel supplied by Naylor and Company of Sheffield, England (via their New York office), agreed to manufacture the weapons. Whitney produced 1100 so-called "Whitneyville-Walker" six-shot pistols. Some of them blew up, but most users of the .44 caliber 4 lb., 9 oz. 9-inch barreled pistols were impressed. Within a year, Colt was able to modify the weapon, and with the promise of more contracts, he negotiated with Whitney to purchase available machinery and parts, and then set up in business on his own at his home town of Hartford, Connecticut. In

1848, following modifications and improvements to the metals used, Sam introduced his Dragoon or Holster pistol. He had cut the barrel back to 7½ inches, and reduced its weight to 4 lbs., 2 ozs. Tests proved it to be a formidable weapon. Loaded with 40 grains of black powder and a soft lead 140 grain bullet, it achieved a muzzle velocity of 1,100 feet per second; but with a 212 grain bullet, this dropped to between 820 and 920 feet per second. In 1854, the British Board of Ordnance tested a Dragoon pistol. Thirty-six shots were fired, using a bench rest, at a six foot square iron target set up 450 yards away, and every ball was found to have struck the target.

Like all Colt's open frame percussion revolvers, it was fitted with "open sights"—either a blade or pin placed at the muzzle end of the barrel and a rear sight that consisted of a "V" cut into the lip of the hammer that lined up with the front sight when the weapon was at full cock. Predictably, the Dragoon's great weight was its downfall, and its use was confined mostly to mounted troops or those hardy enough to tote such a weapon in a belt holster! Nevertheless it was *the* man-stopper of its day and remained so until the appearance of Magnum loads.

Notes

1. E. F. Heisler and D. M. Smith, *Atlas Map of Johnson County Kansas.* Wyandotte, Kansas, 1874, 44.

COLT'S NAVY PISTOL, MODEL 1851

Wild Bill Hickok's attachment to Colt's Navy pistol is understandable, for it was probably the most popular of all Sam Colt's large size percussion or "cap and ball" revolvers. Designed originally about 1847, it owes its origin to the so-called .31 caliber Pocket or "Baby Dragoon" pistol that eventually became the Model of 1849, and which remained in production until 1873.

For the "New Ranger Size Pistol" (in honor of Jack Hays) first produced in 1850 was in effect an enlarged version of the Pocket model. However, it soon lost its "Ranger" status and became immortalized as the "Navy" revolver. Produced in .36 caliber, this six-shot pistol weighed 2 lbs., 10 oz., and with a 7-½-inch octagonal-shaped barrel, it was well balanced. Ordnance tests by both the American and British governments, proved it to be deadly accurate at ranges from fifty to over 200 yards—the latter distances fired from a rest! During tests for penetration, an 83-grain lead bullet, propelled by twenty grains of black power, went through six one-inch pine boards set about an inch apart with considerable force. And on one occasion 1,500 shots were fired from one pistol in a day with only one cleaning to prove its reliability. Not once did it misfire. It should be noted that in these tests, "to reduce recoil," the weapon was underloaded (the cylinder could accept thirty grains of powder).

The decision to discard the "Ranger" definition and replace it by "Navy" has not been found in company records, but many think that it was inspired by the rolled-on engraving around the circumference of the cylinder. This depicted a battle between ships of the Texas Navy and some Mexican vessels, and the date "16 May 1843." This fact, or the pistol's .36 caliber—one that was popular with the U.S. Navy—may have been responsible. Nevertheless, as the "Navy" it soon achieved worldwide fame. Indeed, it was the first revolver to be purchased in bulk (about 25,000) by the British Government for service in the Crimean War. British iron and steel, supplied by Thomas Firth & Sons of Sheffield, was also used in the manufacture of most of Colt's Hartford and London-made weapons, where he had a factory from 1852 until 1857).[1]

By 1851, the Navy was also much in demand in the west, and by the outbreak of the Civil War in 1861, many thousands were in civilian and military hands. Doubtless Hickok and the other scouts and spies were supplied with pistols from store, or perhaps purchased their own—being paid five dollars a day as a scout cum spy was a fortune compared to the 13 dollars a month most soldiers earned—so the cost of a $25 pistol would not stretch Hickok's finances too much. Two photographs of him made during the war (and reproduced in this volume) depict him with normal walnut-stocked pistols, but by early 1867 he was known to be armed with a pair of ivory-handled Navies.

Following the war, the Navy was a common sight on the trails up from Texas or on the streets of the Kansas cowtowns. In 1860 Colt introduced an updated version of the Navy which resembled the New Model Army Pistol of 1860. The octagonal barrel was replaced by a rounded version, and the old hinged rammer/loading lever by a "creeping lever." This functioned by means of ratchets that fitted into holes drilled into the barrel lug. The new Navy, however, did not prove to be as popular as the earlier version, and both models were discontinued in 1873.

Notes

1. This arrangement continued until the late 1860s, the metal being supplied in the bar or part forged. In the late 1850s

Sam began importing their "silver steel" (which had been in used in Europe for many years) which enabled him to produce lighter weapons—notably the New Model Army of 1860 (see: Joseph G. Rosa, *Colonel Colt London,* London, 1976, and "Ricochet"—readers' response to articles—in *Man at Arms,* July/August 1985, for this author's lengthy description of the origins and use of "silver steel.").

COLT'S NEW MODEL ARMY PISTOL, MODEL 1860

Late in the 1850s, with the introduction by Remington and others of .44 caliber weapons that were lighter than his Dragoon pistol, Sam Colt tried to reduce its weight by removing metal from the frame and barrel. This proved unsuccessful, and several disastrous prototypes later, he produced a weapon that was meant to be a stopgap model, but one that was only superseded by the introduction of cartridge weapons.

Colt's experiments with English "silver steel" enabled him cut down the weight of his pistols by reducing the thickness of barrels and the chamber walls of the cylinders.

The "New Model Army Revolver," first produced in 1859 (and later dubbed the "1860 Army") was a modified version of the original Navy revolver, but designed to replace the Dragoon. It never matched the latter's ballistics, but nevertheless proved to be popular and an estimated 127,157 Armys were purchased by the Union government during the Civil War. Colt's engineers, under Sam's supervision, took the original Navy model frame and machined a "step" at the front of its bed to accept a rebated cylinder. Thus the rear portion remained identical to the Navy's in size, but the "stepped down" forepart allowed the engineers to enlarge the front of the cylinder to increase its caliber from .36 to .44. The octagonal barrel was discarded and replaced by a rounded and "streamlined" version. The screwed lever ramrod was also replaced by a "creeping lever" type with teeth or notches that locked into holes machined into the barrel housing. By late 1859 the prototype of the so-called "1860 Army" had undergone tests, and, on Ordnance Department recommendations, its barrel length was increased from 7-1/2" to 8" and its handle lengthened by three eights of an inch. Although its .44 caliber and 40 grains of black powder was in theory ballistically similar to the Dragoon, the new pistol (despite government requested changes) experienced increased recoil—something the mighty Dragoon did not suffer from. The decision was then made to reduce the powder charge to thirty grains for military use, and employ a 216 grain bullet that cut its muzzle velocity back to about 740 feet per second, but it still packed sufficient "punch" to stop someone in their tracks. Civilians, of course, had no such restrictions and most people loaded with a full charge.

Back in 1859-60, however, because so much metal had been machined from the cylinder chambers to accept the .44 bullet, some of the early models blew up (usually around the cylinder bolt notches). Colt solved that problem by making the rear of the chamber conical in shape to provide more metal under the bolt notches. Later, the creeping lever ramrod also caused some problems. This was case-hardened, whereas the barrel and its housing was not which led eventually to much wear and, occasionally, pressure on the lever pushed the ratchets up towards the bore causing indentations in the rifling. But defects of this kind were in the extreme. For the most part the Army suffered from the same problems experienced by all makes of revolver—lack of proper cleaning and neglect which led to rusting and corrosive pitting.

Despite any latent defects, the 1860 Army proved popular with Cavalry regiments and, like the Navy, was also appreciated by mounted horsemen on either side during the Civil War. Following several conversions to early rim- and center-fire ammunition, and some new models based upon the weapon's general design, the original percussion version was discontinued in 1873 to make way for the Peacemaker.[1]

Notes

1. James S. Hutchins, "A Momentary Design Glitch in Colt's New Model," *Man at Arms,* December, 1998, 44-48; John D. McAulay. *Civil War Pistols,* 37.

REMINGTON NEW MODEL ARMY REVOLVER, MODEL 1863

Colt's biggest American rival during the Civil War, and in the immediate postwar years, was the Remington Arms Company of Illion New York. The company could trace its origins back to 1816, and by the mid 1840s had an enviable reputation for long arms. But their fortunes changed dramatically in 1845 when they completed a government contract that another maker had failed to meet. By 1856, when Colt's basic patents were about to run out, Remington decided it was time they, too, produced revolvers. The company employed Fordyce Beals, a professional gun designer, to work on a suitable weapon. His first effort was moderately successful, but the final version, the New Model Army Revolver of 1863, proved to be very popular. Many thousands of them were sold to the Government and, following the war, the 1863 version vied with Colt for civilian and military use.

The basic difference between the Colt .44 caliber Army and the .44 Remington model was that the Colt was open-topped (there is no top strap over the cylinder) whereas the Remington had a solid frame—an unusual feature on American revolvers of the time. A minor lock change on the Remington extended the cylinder bolt so that it and the trigger could be hung on one screw, whereas the Colt had a screw for each part. Rivalry between both makers and models was predictable. The Colt, because of its lack of a top strap and the inclusion of an anti-fouling grease groove on its cylinder arbor, rarely jammed or suffered from cylinder lock due to fouling. The Remington, however, although it could be stripped down faster, was fitted with a small cylinder pin or arbor that lacked a grease groove and soon became fouled, sometimes jamming the cylinder.

In 1864 it was reported by the Ordnance Department that a number of Remington revolvers purchased by contract were sub-standard. It was stated that some of the stocks were made from "green" wood; front sight orifices had been drilled into the bore; slag had been noticed in frames and in general the pistols were unsuitable. Remington offered to buy the weapons back for the civilian market. Similar problems were experienced in the west where misfires or weapons exploding when fired were reported. Some cavalry commanders refused to issue Remingtons. General C. C. Auger, in command of the Department of the Platte, was angered by the situation, and in early 1867 wrote to the Chief of Ordnance, pointing out that his command had not experienced similar problems with Colt's pistols.[1]

Despite its shortcomings, the Remington pistol remained popular and today is much prized by collectors and some shooters. However, back in the 1860s, the fact that some Cavalry regiments (notably some companies of the Seventh) were issued Remingtons proved a boon insofar as Hickok was concerned. When John Kile pulled the trigger of his Remington after pushing its muzzle into Hickok's ear, and it misfired, it allowed Hickok time to draw his Navy and to mortally wound Kile and severely wound his companion Lonergan.

Notes

1. Ordnance Department Records (1861-69), National Archives, Washington, D.C.

SMITH & WESSON NO. 3 "AMERICAN"

Wild Bill's association with Smith & Wesson revolvers stems from his alleged use of a No. 2 .32 caliber tip-up "Army" five shot rim-fire revolver first issued during the Civil War and re-issued in later years. Some claim such a weapon was taken from his body by Seth Bullock (who arrived in Deadwood the day before Hickok was murdered); but there is no real evidence to back that yarn or that such a weapon was ever owned or used by Wild Bill.

However, there is evidence to support the claim that Hickok owned a pair of .44 caliber No. 3's, the "American" Model. In March 1874, when Wild Bill quit Buffalo Bill Cody's Theatrical Combination at Rochester, New York, Cody and Texas Jack Omohundro presented Hickok with $1000 and a pair of No. 3's. His niece, the late Ethel Hickok, once showed the writer an undated news-clipping in her personal scrapbook which stated that Wild Bill had been interviewed in Colorado later that year and was armed with "a pair of heavy Smith & Wesson revolvers, which shoot nearly as accurately as rifles."

Patented in 1869, the No. 3 was unique in that it dispensed with the side loading gate and rod ejection used by Colt and Remington, and employed a facet of many European arms—a hinged barrel with a built-in ejector that ejected spent cartridges when the barrel was "broken." This system facilitated faster loading, but cavalrymen complained that if they only fired a couple of rounds and wished to reload, they had to run the risk of losing the lot if performing the act at a gallop! Nevertheless, the pistol and its successor the New Model No. 3 were popular with many military men and westerners alike.

To date, Wild Bill's pair of Smith & Wessons have not been found, and it seems evident that he did not take them with him on the trip to Deadwood.

WILLIAMSON DERRINGER

Wild Bill, according to several sources, carried a pair of .41 caliber Williamson derringers as backup for his two .36 caliber Colt's Navy revolvers. (Henry Deringer, spelled with one "r," invented a small gun called the "Deringer." Other makers of similar small guns used the generic term "derringer" with two "r's" to avoid legal problems.) Writing in the *Los Angeles Times' Illustrated Weekly* of February 14, 1906, someone signing himself "G.W.S." claimed that his low-cut waistcoat or vest was worn with "the top buttons of the latter garment being always open. Tucked inside this vest were the weapons which were the foundation of Wild Bill's reputation, and which sent many a clever gun man to Boot Hill for burial."

Others, including Bat Masterson, recalled that Hickok carried and used a pair of derringers. In *The Denver Republican* of July 17, 1910, in an article entitled "A Few Scraps," he claimed that during the period Hickok resided in Kansas City in the early 1870s he had been ordered to disarm; but when he was forced to "go skipping past alleys and street corners, especially on dark nights, till you'd take him for a ballet dancer," he obtained permission to carry a pair of derringers—which convinced most people that he should be left alone.

Bat and others, however, failed to identify the derringers, and one enterprising individual claimed to have acquired one of Hickok's derringers—a Hammond "Bulldog" which is now exhibited in an Arkansas museum, but provided no provenance. In the 1950s, I found a reference to the weapons being Williamsons in an unidentified source circa the 1880s.

I mentioned this to my friend the late Raymond W. Thorp, who advised me that he had been aware of one of Hickok's Williamson derringers since the 1920s when it was owned by Guy Clark (whose Hickok connection has previously been discussed), who sold it to Waldo L. Rich, one of Thorp's many friends. Described as being finely engraved, gold-plated and fitted with a fine curly maple stock, Clark said that Buffalo Bill had given the pistol to him. According to the story, Hickok presented it to Cody when the pair met up at Denver in 1875, claiming to have killed 26 men with it! We know that Hickok and Cody did not meet up at Denver in 1875. After they parted at Rochester, New York, in March 1874, they may have met up at Cheyenne that year, or in 1875, but definitely met for the last time at Hat Creek, W. T., on July 6, 1876. When Rich died, Thorp asked his family if he might purchase the Williamson derringer, but they had no idea where it had gone and offered him a Colt No. 3 "Theur" derringer instead which had nothing to do with Wild Bill.

We can dismiss the alleged 26 slayings by Hickok with a deringer, and some of the ridiculous yarns of his marksmanship at 75 yards with one, and say that there is no contemporary evidence to suggest that Hickok ever shot anyone with a derringer. Rather, like many other gamblers, he probably carried one or a pair as backup weapons—ideal when seated!

The Williamson,[1] however, was unique: it was the only multi-ignition derringer available at the time. Most were either percussion (or cap and ball) or chambered for .22, .32, or .41 caliber rim-fire cartridges. The Williamson, although chambered for .41 rim-fire ammunition, could also accept an insert (a metal cartridge case-like tube complete with percussion nipple) which could be loaded with loose powder, ball and a percussion cap. The latter was exploded by a small stud below the rim-fire striker. To enable this to work, the nipple and cap projected into the frame to meet the hammer stud (page 40). But much of the Williamson's appeal was it similarity to the original Henry Deringer pistols, one of which was used by John Wilkes Booth to assassinate Abraham Lincoln on April 14, 1865.

Notes

1. For a detailed description of the Williamson derringer and its variations, *see* "The Williamson: Some Notes on a Famous Dual-Ignition Deringer," by Joseph G. Rosa, *Man at Arms*, (September/October, 1992), 10-18.

BIBLIOGRAPHY

Books and Pamphlets

Buel, J. W. *Heroes of the Plains.* New York and St. Louis, Missouri, 1882.

Connelley, William E. *Wild Bill and His Era.* New York, 1933.

Cunningham, Eugene. *Triggernometry: A Gallery of Gunfighters.* Norman, Oklahoma 1996.

Custer, Gen. George A. *My Life on the Plains.* New York, 1874 and 1876.

Flannery, L. G. ("Pat") (editor) *John Hunton's Diary (1876-77).* Lingle, Wyoming, 1958.

Drees, James D. *Bloody Prairie: Ellis County's Wildest Years 1865-1875.* Hays, Kansas, 1997.

Gard, Wayne. *The Chisholm Trail.* Norman, Oklahoma, 1954.

Dugan, Mark. *Tales Never Told Around the Campfire.* Athens, Ohio, 1990.

Hardin, John Wesley. *The Life of John Wesley Hardin.* Norman, Oklahoma, 1961.

Greener, W. W. *The Gun and its Development.* London, 1910.

Heisler, E. F., and D. M. Smith. *Atlas Map of Johnson County Kansas.* Wyandotte, Kansas, 1874.

Maguire, N. N. *The Coming of Empire: A Complete and Reliable Treatise on the Black Hills, Yellowtone, and Big Horn Regions.* Sioux City, Iowa, 1878.

Marohn, Richard C. *The Last Gunfighter.* College Station, Texas 1995.

Mayer, Frank H., and Charles B. Roth. *The Buffalo Harvest.* Denver, 1958.

McAulay, John D. *Civil War Pistols.* Lincoln, Rhode Island. 1992.

McClintock, John S. *Pioneer Days in the Black Hills.* Deadwood, South Dakota, 1939.

McGivern, Ed. *Fast and Fancy Revolver Shooting.* Chicago, 1975.

Metz, Leon. *John Wesley Hardin: Dark Angel of Texas.* Norman, Oklahoma, 1998.

Roenigk, Adolph. *Pioneer History of Kansas.* Lincoln, Kansas, 1933.

Rosa, Joseph G. *They Called Him Wild Bill: The Life and Adventures of James Butler Hickok.* Norman, Oklahoma, 1964, 1974.

—— *Alias Jack McCall: A Pardon or Death? An Account of the Trial, Petition* for a Presidential Pardon, and Execution of John McCall for the Murder of *Wild Bill Hickok.* Kansas City, Missouri, 1967.

—— *The Gunfighter: Man or Myth?* Norman, Oklahoma, 1969.

—— *The West of Wild Bill Hickok.* Norman, Oklahoma, 1982.

—— *Colonel Colt London.* London, 1976.

—— *Wild Bill Hickok: The Man and His Myth.* Lawrence, Kansas, 1996.

Secrest, William B. (editor) *I Buried Hickok: The Memoirs of White Eye Anderson.* College Station, Texas, 1980.

Spring, Agnes Wright. *Colorado Charley, Wild Bill's Pard.* Boulder, Colorado, 1968.

Taylerson, A. W. F. *The Revolver 1865-1888.* London, 1966.

Thorp, Raymond W. *Spirit Gun of the West—The Story of Doc Carver.* Glendale, California, 1957.

Webb, W. E. *Buffalo Land: An Authentic Narrative of the Adventures and Misadventures of a Late Scientific and Sporting Party upon the Great Plains of the West.* Cincinnati, Ohio, and Chicago, Illinois, 1872.

Young, Harry (Sam). *Hard Knocks: A Life Story of the Vanishing West.* Chicago, Illinois, 1915.

Magazines and Articles

Connelley, William E. "Wild Bill—James Butler Hickok: David C, McCanles at Rock Creek," Kansas State Historical Society's *Collections* 17 (1926-28).

Hansen, George W. "The True Story of Wild Bill-McCanles Affray in Jefferson County, Nebraska, July 12, 1861," *Nebraska History Magazine* (April-June1927).

Hutchins, James S. "A Momentary Design Glitch in Colt's New Model," *Man at Arms* (December, 1998).

Little, Theophilus. "Early Days of Abilene and Dickinson County" (included in Roenigk's *Pioneer History of Kansas*).

McLaird, James D. "Calamity Jane's Diary and Letters, Story of a Fraud," *Montana: The Magazine of Western History* 45:4 (Autumn/Winter 1995).

Nichols, Colonel G. W. "Wild Bill," *Harper's New Monthly Magazine* (February, 1867).

Richardson, Leander P. "A Trip to the Black Hills," *Scribner's Monthly,* Volume. XIII (February, 1877).

Rosa, Joseph G. "George Ward Nichols and the Legend of Wild Bill Hickok," *Arizona and the West* 19:2 (Summer 1977).

——— "J. B. Hickok, Deputy U. S. Marshal." *Kansas History: A Journal of the Central Plains* 2:4 (Winter, 1979).

——— "Ricochet"—Readers' response to articles—on the subject of the origin and use of so-called "silver steel," *Man at Arms,* July/August, 1985.

——— "Little Dave's Last Fight: What Really Happened when Wild Bill Hickok and Davis K. Tutt Shot it out at Springfield, Missouri," National Association for Outlaw and Lawman History's *Quarterly* (October-December 1996).

———"The Williamson: Some Notes on a Famous Dual-Ignition Deringer." *Man at Arms* 14:5 (September/October 1992).

——— "Jack McCall, Assassin: An Updated Account of his Yankton Trial, Plea for Clemency, and Execution." *The Brand Book,* Volume 32, No. 1, Winter 1997/1998 (published 1999), The English Westerners' Society, London.

Sanborn, John B. *The Campaign in Missouri in September and October, 1864.* n.p.n.d., Circa 1890.

Staab, Rodney. "The Matthew Clarkson Manuscripts." *Kansas History: A Journal of the Central Plains. 5:4 (Winter, 1982).*

Thomas, Chauncey, (last interview with Buffalo Bill) *Outdoor Life,* January 1917.

Thorp, Raymond W. "The Pistol *that* Killed Wild Bill," *Trails of the Northwoods* (Summer 1930).

Manuscripts and Other Materials

Barnitz, Maj. Albert, Diary and Journals covering the period 1861-1870 (Barnitz Papers, the Benecke Library, Yale University).

Colt's Patent Fire Arms Manufacturing Company to Joseph G. Rosa, September 18, 1957.

Court Records: These include the McCanles case (Nebraska State Historical Society);

The Tutt Killing (Greene County Archive, Springfield, Mo.); Records relative to Hickok's services as a Deputy U. S. Marshal (National Archives, Kansas City, Missouri, and payments received are located in Washington; The McCall Case records are housed at Kansas City, and his Pardon File (No. F-307, Records Group No. 204) are on file in Washington).

Gross, Charles F. to J. B. Edwards (1922-1926 correspondence). Manuscripts Division, Kansas State Historical Society.

Harvey, Winfield S. Typed copy of his diary in Container 6, the Edward S. Godfrey Papers, Library of Congress, Washington, D.C.

Jones & Cartwright, Leavenworth, Kansas, to Horace A. Hickok, June 6, 1861. Author's Collection.

Ordnance Department Records. National Archives, Washington, D.C.

Philip, W. D. Notes on Matt Clarkson. Manuscripts Division, Kansas State Historical Society.

Records of the Quartermaster General, Civilians Hired as Scouts, Couriers and Teamsters for the period 1861-1870. National Archives, Washington, D.C.

Smith, William B. Statement made to H. L. Humphrey, February 1932, on the Coe killing and early days in Abilene. University of Kansas Collections, Lawrence, Kansas.

Newspapers

These are listed by name; the dates cited are mentioned in the text.

Abilene (Kansas) *Chronicle*

Atchison (Kansas) *Daily Champion*

Austin (Texas) *Weekly State Journal*

Burlingame (Kansas) *Weekly Osage Chronicle*

Burlington (Iowa) *The Daily Hawkeye*

Cheyenne (Wyoming Territory) *Daily Leader*

Cheyenne (Wyoming Territory) *Daily News*

Cheyenne (Wyoming Territory) *Daily Sun*

Chicago (Illinois) *Inter-Ocean*

Chicago (Illinois) *Tribune*

Clyde (Kansas) *Republican Valley Enterprise*

Deadwood (Dakota Territory) *Black Hills Daily Pioneer*

Deadwood (Dakota Territory) *Black Hills Pioneer Times*

Deadwood (Dakota Territory) *Black Hills Daily Times*

Denver (Colorado) *Denver News*

Dodge City (Kansas) *Ford County Republican*

Hays City (Kansas) *Ellis County Star*

Junction City (Kansas) *Daily* and *Weekly Union*

Kansas City (Missouri) *Daily Journal of Commerce*

Laramie (Wyoming Territory) *Daily Chronicle*

Lawrence (Kansas) *Daily Tribune*

Lawrence (Kansas) *Republican Journal*

Lawrence (Kansas) *State* Journal

Leavenworth (Kansas) *Appeal*

Leavenworth (Kansas) *Commercial*

Leavenworth (Kansas) *Times and Conservative*

Mendota (Illinois) *Bulletin*

Newton (Massachusetts) *Circuit*

Oxford (Kansas) *Times*

Rochester (New York) *Democrat and Chronical*

Springfield *Weekly Missouri Patriot*

Saint Louis (Missouri) *Daily Democrat*

Saint Paul (Minnesota) *Pioneer Press and Tribune*

Topeka (Kansas) *Daily Commonwealth*

Topeka (Kansas) *North Topeka Times*

West Chester (Pennsylvania) *Daily Local News*

Wichita (Kansas) *Eagle*

Wichita (Kansas) *Weekly Beacon*

Wyandotte (Kansas) *Gazette*

Yankton (Dakota Territory) *Press and Dakotaian*

Yankton (Dakota Territory) *Dakota Herald*

INDEX